herb/a cook's companion

For Candida, who loves herbs beyond what's normal.

Publishing Director Sarah Lavelle
Junior Commissioning Editor Harriet Webster
Head of Design Claire Rochford
Design Matt Cox at Newman+Eastwood Ltd.
Cover Design Composition by Matt Cox from original illustrations by Tatiana Boyko
Photographer Mark Diacono
Food Stylists Matt Williamson and Mark Diacono
Head of Production Stephen Lang
Production Controller Sinead Hering

Published in 2021 by Quadrille, an imprint of Hardie Grant Publishing

Quadrille
52–54 Southwark Street
London SE1 1UN
quadrille.com

Cataloguing in Publication Data: a catalogue record for this book is available from the British Library.

text © Mark Diacono 2021
photography © Mark Diacono 2021
design © Quadrille 2021

ISBN 978 1 78713 635 9

Printed in China

herb/a cook's companion

MARK DIACONO

Hardie Grant

QUADRILLE

CONTENTS

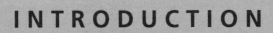

INTRODUCTION

I'm sitting within an incomplete ring of pots, each full of herbs, their flowers alive with pollinators, the sun flashing bright as I scribble. It's the middle of summer and most are plump and at their oily peak; some letting the sun draw flowers skyward, others pregnant with buds. A few – like the lemongrass that has scented my fingers – are invisibly becoming more themselves in the heat, intensifying in flavour and scent as if knowing that's exactly what we want of them. On days like this, their beauty and scent are enough to make this non-believer ponder the presence of an all-guiding hand.

If you were sitting here, you'd recognize many. A few are variations on a familiar theme: there's orange thyme, ginger rosemary, and Thai basil, its leaves bright with spicy nutmeg scent. I can brush three lemon verbenas without moving. To my left, a pair of lavenders: one that's best for the kitchen, another that's bordering on the fabric softener but beautiful to me and the bees. Just behind, summer savory, resinous as a creosoted fence and an ever-closer friend these last few years; I've come to love its slightly bitter tones, especially when end-of-season tomatoes need bringing into line in the hottest of ovens or over an outdoor fire. Next to it, the Vietnamese coriander I feel I've got to know since I stopped being too influenced by its name: yes, it is a bright, lemony version of coriander's familiar scent and flavour, but it is so much more too.

There are a few – that bergamot by my foot, for one – that I know I haven't got the best from yet, but that's half the fun. After decades of this – designing kitchen gardens, growing and using an almost impossible variety of herbs at Otter Farm, at River Cottage and in this small garden – I'm still scratching the surface. I like that. As much as I love a brilliant book reaching a satisfying conclusion, I want parts of my life to stay open-ended, to be an inexhaustible pleasure, and herbs are just that.

Whether in the garden or kitchen, herbs are elevators; transporters engaging us in a way that a potato or a cauliflower, however glorious, cannot hope to. Using them is a sensory experience often indivisible into its constituents. So very often, their flavour and scent are interwoven; you can intuit how they might inform your cooking by rubbing their leaves and paying attention to what the smell tells you. It goes further: the dark leaves of Chocolate mint smell cold; my daughter swears lavender tastes purple. I know what she means.

This characteristic also allows herbs to carry other ingredients more deeply into the senses. Take the mojito, that holy alliance of rum, lime, sugar, soda and mint, so right that it makes this unconvinced man think of the occasional brilliance of our flawed species. And it is the mint that laces the shoe for the lime and rum to kick you so very perfectly in the consciousness.

Herbs' elevating quality is really just awaiting your exploration. Mint with lemon verbena, dill and salmon, sorrel and new potatoes, lovage and Lancashire cheese; these mark the merest tip of the herbal iceberg. You don't even have to try to be clever with herbs: they offer a wealth of clothes for even the simplest ingredients to dress up in. A panful of just-cooked new potatoes are wildly, deliciously different depending on whether you cast in a handful of sorrel or mint or a sliver of lovage.

Understanding a little about herbs goes a long way towards making the best of them. Herbs fall into two camps: perennials that endure for years, and annuals that are sown, grown and eaten within a year. Many perennials – sage, rosemary, thyme – are woody plants with glossy leaves that are resistant to tooth and knife; annuals – parsley, coriander and basil – are usually softer, easily torn, chewed and chopped. A few, such as mint and chives, are perennials with soft leaves.

The woodier perennial herbs should be high on any cook's list of favourites to grow; aside from their flavour, they are easy and pickable every day of the year. Many are not eaten, as such, but rather lend their flavour to whatever they are with. Bay and scented geraniums are among those that give up so much to alcohol, sugar syrup, water, milk or cream, but eating the leaves is to eat the wrapper rather than the sweet. There are exceptions: counter-intuitively, the cat's tongue of a sage leaf becomes glorious fried to a crackle, and rosemary chopped to a pile of full stops brings flavour without the usual barbs.

For most of the soft herbs, the Hippocratic oath applies: first, do no harm. In general, the less you have to do with their soft, thin leaves from the moment they leave the plant until you taste them, the better. While heat can be your friend with woody herbs, it can completely destroy soft herbs' precious scent and flavour, hence reaching for them almost always indicates that I am about to walk from oven to table.

Of course, this is a spectrum rather than a sharp distinction. Warmth can unlock so much in soft herbs that heat kills: fridge-cold pesto may as well be chain oil, yet under only the warmth that pasta is willing to let go, it sings. A few of the more robust soft herbs such as lovage can take some cooking. Those often-discarded, untasted stems of coriander are full of extraordinary flavour and can stand up to oily heat, their flavour enriching the base of a soup that a last-minute scattering of the leaves talks to. Complexity, interest and flavour results.

This sea of pleasure is ours to dive into. Even in the supermarket the range of herbs is ever-increasing: this morning I found lemon thyme, lovage and Thai basil in my nearest, each absent only a few years ago. Those supplying direct through box schemes, farmers' markets and farm shops offer an even greater range. Online suppliers invite us to use herbs – fresh and dried – from other cultures and cuisines. Plant nurseries push open the doors of flavour possibility even further. I join their chorus.

So much of what follows is about getting herbs' flavour pleasingly across your taste buds. A lot of it is to do with timing; how you use your knife is crucial. Some of it is about using fats, salt, sugar and liquids to draw out and carry the flavour of herbs that are best infused, about appreciating their varying affinities with citrus, chilli, garlic, oil and other harmonious partners. I will tell you what I know and encourage you to explore further.

The **Herb Skills** chapter will guide you through all you need to get the best from herbs in the kitchen, to capture their flavour, to preserve them, to know how and when to add them. It has all the principles you need to grow herbs too, and I hope you'll be moved to try growing even a few – it will improve your life in endless, tiny measures.

Herbs to Grow and Eat builds on that, focusing on dozens of extraordinary herbs. For the most part, using them well is laughably easy; you just have to become familiar with how to make each sing and you will become a better cook. I will help you to be bold and use herbs with exuberance, as well as finesse. I will invite you to try new flavours. I will encourage you to look at the herbs you already use with fresh eyes, as it's easy to take the familiar for granted.

I have two aims with this book: to encourage you – whether lacking in confidence and inexperienced, or already using herbs inquisitively – to step beyond your safe zone and explore the delicious possibilities, and to persuade and cajole you into growing even a few of the easiest herbs for yourself. Both are undeniably life-enhancing and, for many, life-changing.

HERB SKILLS

IN THE GARDEN

There is great pleasure in growing a plant, in picking a few flavoursome leaves from a living thing that grows more to replace those you take. It is a tiny, doorstep microcosm of the symbiosis on which our species depends. Most herbs are easy to grow and require little of your time: you aren't waiting for fruit, or that fleeting moment of perfect form as you are with a cauli, nor is your harvest a single picking; the leaves are the prize and the plant's job is to grow them to survive.

One of the pleasures of growing herbs is that it is a relatively straightforward affair. Many have particularities – they may prefer sun or shade, a drier soil or plentiful watering – but they want to grow and there is little you have to do to help them. Unlike with vegetables, there's no crop rotation to worry about, there are fewer pests and diseases, and many herbs either self-seed or are perennial and produce for years. Do the few crucial things well and it is very likely that you will have repeated handfuls of big flavours to elevate your meals.

Key principles apply: most herbs enjoy sunshine and like to be out of the harshest winds, and while almost all like a good amount of water through the growing season, they favour growing in a fairly well-drained soil. Where there is an anomaly to the norm – a herb that loves damp soil, or one that prefers shade – I've noted that in the Herbs to Grow and Eat section.

Your soil type is worth getting to know, just a little: if it holds together when squeezed into a sausage shape when wet it is likely to be fairly clayey and adding some grit and/or compost will improve drainage. Where the soil is sandy and free-draining, compost provides fibre and body to help retain water as well as provide nutrients. A soil pH testing kit is a useful and easy thing to use: a crumbling of soil is tested in a tube and if your soil is somewhere towards the central band of 6–7 on the scale (as it almost certainly will be) it will be perfect for almost all herbs, vegetables and fruit. If it's markedly away from this happy medium, compost will, in effect, dilute it away from the extreme and towards the centre. As you can see, compost is always the answer.

Where you can, work in harmony with the conditions: sunny, sandy and well drained is ideal for the 'Mediterranean' herbs such as rosemary and lavender, so plant them there; if you have shadier, damper, heavier locations, that's where angelica, sweet cicely and others will thrive.

Should your soil be truly compromised, you can overcome its limitations either by creating a raised bed or by using containers. Here you control everything, from the growing medium, to how you feed your plants, to their location and, if in containers, you can even bring your herbs under cover or into shade should they need protection from seasonal variations.

If you are a beginner, I'd suggest starting with a few perennial herbs: they have established roots, and your job is largely ensuring they have the soil, position and water they need and perhaps shifting them up a pot size once in a while. As the old building site phrase goes: if you can piss, you can paint; growing perennial herbs is similar. They produce for years, are easy to propagate from cuttings (pages 17–18) and require little watering in winter.

Expertise is not required, just a willingness to read the few lines attached to each herb in the Herbs to Grow and Eat section. Just do the very few simple things – as straightforward as putting sausages in the fridge until you cook them – and they will provide.

Space isn't an issue. Everything in this book grows happily in a container, so even a patch of concrete can be a flourishing garden. A few pots can fill you with wonder and change every meal you eat. Start small, go for the easiest, do the right things and build from there: confidence and momentum are the mothers of success.

There is another reason to grow herbs: many are beautiful to the eyes and nose. Anise hyssop in flower, lovage in seed, the early flowers and seeds of sweet cicely and even the tiny white flowers of lemon thyme can lift the soul. Even a few container herbs will draw pollinators and other beneficial insects into the garden.

Choosing what to grow

Having spent much of the last quarter of a century growing hundreds of edible plants – everything from peas to pecans – I feel overqualified in offering some thoughts about what you might grow.

- Consider what you already have. If you can source particular herbs from growers, friends and shops, then prioritize growing others. What grows wild in your area? Wild garlic, pineapple weed and oregano are among those you may be able to forage for. I'm obviously not advising you do this, but there are those who pinch the odd rosemary or bay leaf from the plants growing in the supermarket car park rather than buying the ones in packets inside.

- Identify your favourites. Like your favourite albums, you may find they get a less frequent airing than others, but are no less precious for it.

- Which herbs do you eat most? Unless you have much space, it may be sensible to buy them – for me, this is coriander and parsley – and free up space for growing a greater variety of other herbs.

- Open the larder door a little. Orange thyme, Scotch lovage, Korean mint and ginger rosemary are just the tip of the unbuyable iceberg. Each is extraordinary, carrying scent and flavour I wouldn't be without, and there are many others you have to grow yourself to enjoy. Salad burnet, English mace, sweet cicely, rose scented geranium and so on.

- Consider the easiest herbs. Mint requires repeated, premeditated attempts on its life, and still it comes back. Plant bay and rosemary in favourable conditions and the likelihood is they'll thrive. There are more, and I tell you what little they need in the pages tht follow. If I can do it, so can you.

Starting off herbs

Start annual herbs from seed, and most perennial herbs from young plants. Annuals are generally not around long enough to justify the outlay on plants, while buying perennials sidesteps the trickiest, early stage of their life. That said, once you have confidence there is much pleasure to be had in growing new plants from old, and it is a fairly straightforward undertaking.

Below, some general principles that should help; check the Herbs to Grow and Eat pages for detail and anomalies.

Growing from seed

Most herbs can be started from seed in small pots or trays. While warmth is needed for germinating most seeds, sunlight is not, hence most seeds should be covered with compost when sowing. A heated propagator set to 20°C (68°F) will suit most as a steady heat source, but an airing cupboard is an excellent substitute. A warm windowsill will almost always work too.

The growing medium is important. A peat-free organic seed compost is ideal for most herb seeds. A minimum of 5cm (2in) depth of compost for starting off seeds is usual. Generally seeds prefer to be just covered with compost; it should be moist but not overwatered. Some herbs can take time to germinate; be patient.

Once germinated, good light is crucial. In the absence of a greenhouse or similar, a sunny windowsill works well; seedlings should be turned once a day to prevent them growing too hard towards the light. The initial pair of leaves – known as seed leaves – will look unlike those of the plant you are growing; the true leaves that follow will be reassuringly familiar.

Once well into spring, you can direct sow (sowing seed straight into prepared soil) many herbs.

Planting out

When your seedlings are ready to go to their final position, do a little prep first. For a few days, put the seedlings outside in the day and bring them back in at night to allow them to 'harden off'. Seedlings should be watered ahead of planting. Ensure the ground is well prepared, weed-free and in a fairly friable, loose crumb to welcome the growing roots: dig a larger hole than is required to ensure the roots can easily grow into the soil. Water in well, and in subsequent weeks while it gets established.

Propagation

The art of creating children from a parent plant is a rare pleasure that fails to dilute with repetition. The wonder compounds. There are a number of ways of propagating, some more suited to particular herbs than others: refer to Herbs to Grow and Eat to see how best to propagate each.

Cuttings

Many woody perennial herbs like rosemary can be multiplied by taking cuttings. This is so impossibly simple and rewarding that you'd be mad not to try it. In late spring and early summer, when the plant is driving new growth, pull away a new shoot from a stem that's not flowering. It should come with a slender finger from the main stem at its base. Remove all the leaves bar the uppermost few and sink the stem deeply into a mix of potting compost and sand. Secure a clear plastic bag over the pot using an elastic band or string, and make a couple of holes in the bag to create a humid environment with a little ventilation. Place the pot somewhere warm, out of direct sunlight, and keep the compost moist. Remove the bag after three weeks, when the first tiny roots should've established. Keep the compost moist, and pot on or plant out any time from the following spring.

Cuttings can be made from most perennial herbs – including mint, rosemary, thyme and sage – in the spring when the growth is soft, or as semi-hardwood cuttings taken towards the end of the growing season.

Root cuttings

A few herbs – mint and tarragon in particular – can be propagated by root cuttings. The subterranean runners they send out can be cut where you see a small growing node (this is obvious to the eye), and these roots then planted in a seed tray, covered with compost and watered: it may take time, but a new plant should emerge. Spring is the best time for this.

Division

Some herbs crowd themselves out by clumping or forming a mat; do them a favour by dividing them. Chives and oregano are among those that should be split every few years. Depending on their size, a sharp spade, knife or trowel right through the core of the plant should result in two, three or even four refreshed plants. Each piece should be replanted or potted. Division is usually best carried out in spring or after flowering in late summer.

Buying herb plants

Don't buy plants where you buy light bulbs. Go to those who do it for a living. You wouldn't be the first to buy a glowing, leafy, abundant plant to then find it withers in your company; these marvellous-looking specimens have often been grown under considerable heat with endless feed, and are woefully unprepared for the harsh realities of life in the outdoors.

A good specialist nursery (page 266) will provide you with superb plants, grown for a long life rather than just an instant impact, and the pleasure of plants arriving in the post never wears off.

Container growing

Space needn't be an issue. Even when I had 17 acres at my disposal, most of the herbs were grown in containers within a few steps of the door. I don't want to walk far for a little tarragon for the chicken or chervil for an omelette, and neither will you.

Herbs are well suited to growing in containers: mints can spread laterally, which may be what you want to cover ground and give you a large harvest, but if not, container growing is ideal for them. Tender herbs such as lemongrass and lemon verbena can be moved indoors for winter more easily if in containers.

Container growing sidesteps issues of soil, space or location. Most herbs will grow enthusiastically in pots, trugs and other vessels given the right conditions. It is a way of growing that suits beginners and those who have been gardening for decades equally.

The journey to fully grown plant requires a series of pots. You don't have to buy these all at once; as you move a medium-sized plant into a larger pot, it frees up the medium-sized pot for a smaller plant to move into. Don't overpot a plant (i.e. plant a small herb in a large pot) as this is a waste, not only of compost but its nutrients, which will leach away before the plant can take them in. Move plants up a pot size at a time (two at most) until they reach their optimum size. Peat-free organic potting compost is usually ideal, offering a balanced, well-drained growing medium.

The convenience of container growing comes with a little effort. A few tall growers such as lovage and fennel may need staking, and their long roots require deep containers for them to thrive. Feeding is essential, see overleaf.

Pictured opposite: mint that's gone to flower, in winter.

Care
Pruning
Pruning is the art of trimming plants for looks, health and productivity. Woody herbs need to be pruned at certain times; this is easy but the specifics are important, and covered in the Herbs to Grow and Eat section. Annual herbs are productive for a few months and pruning isn't necessary.

A hungry gardener and the inquisitive cook rarely have to worry about their herbs becoming leggy as the plant will be tamed by frequent harvesting, but when not, a little trimming can make a big difference, as straggly plants can slow productivity and flowering can dramatically change the flavour and scent of the leaves. Stay on top of this by snipping out the tops to encourage new growth and dissuade flowering. Of course, some herb flowers – chives are a perfect example – are delicious in themselves or at least don't detrimentally affect the herb's flavour, so by all means let them grow.

Watering
We gardeners dispense love from a watering can, occasionally in stifling amounts.

Most soil-grown perennial herbs require little once established; the exceptions – sweet cicely and lovage among them – will get along perfectly well with little watering if planted in the shadier, moist-soil conditions they prefer. Annual herbs have to go from seed to peak in a short season of growth, throwing down a whole root system and pushing up leaves, stems, flowers, and very possibly fruit and seed in a brief window; typically, they need plenty of love. Specifics are in Herbs to Grow and Eat .

For herbs grown in a container, consideration is needed: their roots' resources are limited, and more frequent watering and feeding is likely. A useful rule of thumb is to test the water just below the surface of the compost; it should be slightly moist.

Timing is important. Water in the morning: slugs do much of their work in the late evening and prefer damp conditions, so I avoid watering then, whereas midday watering can lead to evaporation and leaf scorch. That said, if the only time you have is away from morning, water anyway. Water the soil/compost rather than the plant itself, where possible: this gets the water to the roots quickly and with little waste, and there are some – basil especially – that react badly to having wet leaves. For the most part, herbs need little watering through the colder months.

A water butt is the garden equivalent of making jam: it's the perfect way of conserving gluts to use when you fancy. It is such a great resource if you have a fair number of plants: the water from it will be free and using it helps conserve tap water. Avoid using softened tap water as the high salt content suits few plants.

Feeding
If you want to be a good gardener, focus on looking after the soil more than the plant. Compost is the answer to almost everything. Add a layer of compost around the base of perennial herbs at least once a year. It delivers nutrients and organic matter, improves drainage and yet also has water-holding capacity where needed, and helps promote the activity of beneficial organisms, all while recycling kitchen waste, and making you a kind of above-ground regenerative earthworm, and there are few bigger compliments I can give.

Watering containers leaches some of the nutrients; replenishing that resource by feeding helps keep your herbs thriving. Little and often is best – I use a liquid feed every fortnight or so through the growing season. Homemade feed is simple to make – it's just shredded comfrey and/or nettle leaves left to moulder in a little water until it smells like something with a very poor diet that died a very unpleasant death a very long time ago, that's then diluted with water until it looks as pale as cheap lager. This conveys a broad dose of nutrients to the plant in the small, water-soluble state it finds easiest to take in. Organic chicken manure pellets are another superb option: they sit on the soil or compost surface, gradually releasing their goodness over the season.

Picking herbs

Pick herbs close to when you want to use them, ensuring as much of their flavour and scent makes it into your food as possible. How you harvest can influence the shape, productivity and even the flavour of the herb. Generally speaking, if you pinch out the highest few inches of growth it will encourage a bushier plant to form, restrict the potential for legginess and flowering and give you more leaves for the kitchen.

The flavour and scent of many herbs is most intense as buds are forming. As they fall over the cliff into flowering some of this is lost, especially in the soft, annual herbs, so even if you aren't going to use what you pick, keep them trimmed and shy of flowering. There are exceptions, of course – anise hyssop, sweet cicely and Korean mint are just three of the many that have flowers and seeds that are wonderful to eat. Most perennial herbs, the woodier types such as rosemary and thyme especially, can flower without much impact on their flavour. Herbs to Grow and Eat has more detail on each.

If, like me, you are the sort to prevaricate over everything, from adopting a new fitness regime that will at last turn you into a specimen worthy of objectifying, to what to do on your day off, you may take some persuading to grow herbs for the first time. If that's you, hop to the recipes, and I'll take a bet that you'll venture back to these early pages eventually, because flavour and pleasure always win, in the end.

IN THE KITCHEN

It's important for the cook to understand what the gardener already knows: that herbs are as much a scent as a flavour. The cook's job is to capture, coax and occasionally strangle from their leaves, stems and flowers the best of what they have to offer. Mostly it's a case of not cocking up what's already there awaiting a gentle hand. Your job is to let the herb sing, to take it as quickly and sensitively from plot to plate in such a way that the best of its qualities come out on the plate.

Knowing what to look for when buying herbs – simple but important – sets the parameters for all that follows. How you store them (page 24) has a considerable influence on the vitality, flavour and nutrient status of your herbs, and there are numerous ways of capturing and/or extracting the flavour of herbs at their peak in the pages that follow. Perhaps surprisingly, the simple act of chopping can be the most transformative of all the processes you take herbs through (page 24).

Of course, a glut can encourage you to preserve those fine flavours for another time, even if that's half an hour later. Salt, sugar, vinegar, butter and oil are some of the vehicles for capturing and preserving herbs; for the very great part, the jars and bottles that result are full of something far beyond the necessity of preservation. They are a symphony of flavours, textures and possibilities to be deployed when the mood takes.

Buying fresh and dried herbs

Most of us are reliant on supermarkets for some of our food, and thankfully the quality and range of herbs available there is increasing. That said, farmers' markets, local food outlets, box schemes and independents on the high street are still where you are likely to source the best quality and widest variety of herbs. You may even be able to strike up a conversation with the grower or someone who at least knows them. This is a wonderful thing, shortening the chain on which our existence depends, enriching both the local economy and our social interactions, and it's very likely to lead to you getting more of what you want to eat. Be chatty and inquisitive: growing can be a lonely business and positive interaction can make a huge difference. The place I get parsley and coriander now offers blackcurrant sage, lemon thyme, lovage and Thai basil, having been nagged into supplying me – and now others – with some. Everybody wins.

The parameters of flavour and pleasure are set the moment you buy your herbs. If you can, open a bunch of herbs to examine those at the centre for freshness as much as those on the outside. If they are herbs that should be immediately aromatic (e.g. thyme), smell them! Trust your nose and eyes.

I almost always wash fresh herbs I've not grown, swishing them under a running tap, colander beneath for escapees, before patting dry.

Some herbs are hard to source. Lemon verbena, Vietnamese coriander, fenugreek and so on are rarely in the shops: you have to buy from one of the excellent sources online (page 266), or if you are fortunate to live near either supermarkets aimed at particular communities (there is an outstanding Thai and a Chinese supermarket near me) or in a neighbourhood where the greengrocer has demand for herbs popular in the cuisine of particular cultures, you can find them there. Or grow them yourself.

Most dried herbs disappoint; a few are excellent. Online sources are superb for the exceptional dried herbs: go in search of the dehydrated excellence of Mexican oregano, epazote (which is frankly grim undried), and beyond, using the suppliers listed on page 266.

Storing herbs
Herbs can deteriorate quickly, and knowing how to keep them in prime condition for the longest period is good knowledge.

Buying well (page 22) is the first step. For all soft and most woody herbs, storing them with their stems in a glass of water works wonders. Cut the stem ends of all but the freshly cut, and stand the herbs no more than 6cm (2½in) into the water. Top up as required, keeping them out of strong sunlight and away from sources of heat. If this is impractical, wrapping the ends of a bunch in wet kitchen paper and tying a plastic bag around them extends their life considerably. Most herbs do well if placed in sealed containers or freezer bags in the fridge, unwashed to ensure the leaves are dry and to prevent mould and darkening.

Paradoxically, sealed bags of herbs from the shops should be opened before storing to allow air circulation as the leaves are often a little moist and this helps extend their life. Dry woody herbs will survive for a week or more; soft herbs usually a little less. If you refresh soft herbs in a bowl of cold water for half an hour or so, pat them thoroughly dry and store them in an airtight container in the fridge, they can last for up to a fortnight.

Basil turns black and slippery more quickly in the fridge than out. Chives are the great deceiver: even days-old they look as spritely as when they were cut, but their flavour caught the first train out of town, so pick them as you need them and use bought ones asap.

For gluts or pleasure, making vinegars, oils or any of the other preserving techniques has much to recommend it.

The art of chopping
Chopping is often undertaken absentmindedly, reducing herbs to something resembling loose tea in the dash to serve. We are missing a trick here.

There are two reasons for taking a knife to herbs: to alter the texture, and to affect how we experience the flavour. I suspect that, for the most part, people run a knife through herbs in the same way every time they use them – regardless of whether it's coriander or parsley, whether it's for salsa or soup – and reduce the leaves to their personal standard that's somewhere towards the relatively small. This is perfectly fine, but if you are reading this you are in search of more.

The sharpness of your knife is an ingredient. Care about it. Sharpen it as near to every time you go to chop herbs as real life allows. Leaves should be cut, not scored: anything other than a clean cut will squash and bruise the herb, releasing flavour into your chopping board rather than your mouth.

The grade of cut has huge influence over how your food tastes. Finely chopped herbs tend to add a general impression of themselves to a dish – so a curry might seem nicely 'coriandered', whereas a quick run-through with a single pass of the knife – I'm talking about 3–4 chops per inch – will leave an entirely different impression on the tongue. With this coarser 'confetti' chop, you're likely to experience intermittent bursts of big flavour punctuating inconsistently throughout as each larger fragment is more likely to be chewed and release more of itself in the mouth.

Knowing when not to chop is a skill to acquire, too: whole parsley leaves make a glorious salad leaf; a basil leaf a wrapper for burrata; lovage wrapped around crumbly cheese, and more.

Consider whether you intend to actually eat the herb before using it in a recipe: roast lamb cooked with rosemary is a much more pleasurable experience if you either leave the filament leaves attached to its skewer-like stem to remove on serving, or chop very finely; anything in between is like picking up a dropped box of pins.

The guide below is my attempt at thinking of the spectrum of 'whole' to 'dust' in understandable transitions that influence the flavour of the dish.

Whole
Occasionally, a whole herb leaf is perfect: a sun-warm cherry tomato wrapped in a single basil leaf is as perfect a definition of summer as the phut of opening a new tube of tennis balls, or a lunchtime G&T by a clear, chalk river. The salad on page 158 will, I hope, also convince the sceptical of the excellence of parsley as a salad leaf.

Confetti
Imagine your chopping board covered in leaves as the page of a book and chop it so that you could, with some difficulty and much grumbling, piece the page back together if someone paid you to: this is the level of chop we are looking for here. Pieces of leaf might be 5–9mm (¼–½in) across. (Pictured on page 26.)

Fine chop
Depending on your natural degree of patience, whether you have spent time in a professional kitchen and your general level of cooking, a fine chop might mean anything from just below the dimensions of confetti to a coarse dust. Developing good knife skills – that rocking motion, supported by a hand towards the point on the knife's spine – are easily acquired and practice will find you quickly able to create something finer should you wish, that will convey a general essence of that herb to the dish.

Chiffonade
A chiffonade involves rolling herbs into a cigar shape and shredding finely across in parallel lines, producing filaments that 'soften' coarse leaves such as makrut lime and mint, and is a fine way of cutting soft herbs such as basil and lovage into a middle ground between finely and coarsely chopped. These filaments look good on the plate too, and provide dashes of flavour punctuation in a similar way to confetti. (Pictured on page 27.)

I have to say, I'm not interested in tearing herbs: the leaves end up bruised, in ridiculously irregular pieces that please no one. And let's draw a dark veil over the idea of whole mint leaves: all but the tiniest are an unwelcome nuisance, delivering the texture of a cat's tongue in bursts that are overpowering if the mint has anything about it. And if it hasn't, it has no business being on your plate.

Drying herbs

I dry few herbs, but those I do become as precious as those I use fresh. Lemon verbena, mint, fig leaves and summer savory are particular favourites. It is a cruel trick that many of the herbs that dry best – rosemary, thyme and some of the other perennials – are those available fresh from the plant all year round. That said, they grow more slowly in the cold months, and drying can be a fine way to smooth the curve of summer abundance into leaner times.

I find most others a weak impersonation of their fresh incarnation, an OK cover of a favourite song that makes you crave the original all the more. There are exceptions – dried epazote is Jimi's 'All Along the Watchtower', to Bob's fresh mediocrity.

Soft herbs tend to take less well to drying. Much of their oils, flavours and scents are lost in the process. Mint, chervil and Vietnamese coriander are happy exceptions, becoming in essence different ingredients to fresh, and each has its place.

Drying will not elevate poor herbs. Use herbs at their peak, harvested on a dry day, ideally just before flowering, when a little sun has fallen on them.

There are a few techniques to employ, depending on circumstance. The woody herbs and some others such as mint can be dried by hanging them, as if the ceiling is romantically extending an inverted bouquet to the floor, for a few days/weeks until crisp. Some strip the leaves from the stems to store; I'm too lazy and use them quickly enough not to have noticed any deterioration in not jarring them. An airing cupboard or the very lowest of slightly open ovens will slowly remove the water while leaving the oils intact. A dehydrator is a fantastic way of accelerating the process and perhaps the best way of capturing basil and mint by drying. The moment to stop is when the leaves retain greenery and perfume but are crisp.

Freezing herbs

Most woody herbs freeze well as they are, but soft leaves are best blended with just enough water to create a paste and freeze as ice cubes, or chopped and frozen under a little water in ice-cube trays. The stems of soft herbs, finely chopped and frozen in small tubs or freezer bags, retain their glorious essence, ready to be added to soups, pizzas or wherever you want intense herbiness that will be cooked for a while to soften their texture. Doing this is such a great way of ensuring the stems are used, when they might otherwise go to waste.

Herb salts

Why not just add salt and fresh herbs to the dish? Well, aside from the convenience of reaching for a generous pinch when the urge strikes, herb salts capture the leaves' flavour at its peak, allowing you to enjoy it out of its seasonal cycle, offering flavour without the leafiness, and you don't always have time to run to the garden for thyme, sage or oregano, when finishing a steak or for the final squiggle over darkening halloumi. This is when you'll be glad you banked a few minutes of summer to pay out in winter.

There are a few methods of making herb salt. You can combine dried herbs with salt; this works perfectly well for the herbs like epazote, that shine when dried. For fresh herbs, I have a core method with two punchlines that I employ depending on time and the flavour I'm after. A coffee/spice grinder is borderline indispensable here, as a handful of leaves and salt can be reduced to a fine, wet snow in a moment, whereas a mortar and pestle leaves a less consistent result, although the pleasure of using it is quite the compensation.

You can use herb salt immediately – it's likely to be bright and fresh – though the process needn't stop at this point and I almost never use it the moment it's made. The act of drying is effectively an ingredient here, the flavour elements intensifying into the salt as the water evaporates. *How* you dry the herb salt makes a real difference. Low temperature oven-drying drives the water off quickly and gently to leave an intense, fresh, bright salt; whereas left to air-dry on a sunny windowsill, herb salt develops a fine flavour with similar qualities, yet a slightly seaweedy backbeat. Both are superb, and in a perfect world you might keep both versions for when one best suits; mostly, I zap up a quick batch to go in a cooling post-roast oven, or sit on the windowsill if the oven's not on.

There are a few principles to follow.

- Use coarse salt: it provides the boxing gloves that pound the herbs into a wet green powder.

- Make small batches using 50–60g (2–2½oz) salt; this way you'll get through it relatively quickly while it has peak flavour.

- Put the herbs in the grinder first as the salt will weigh the leaves into the blades.

- If not using the salt immediately, spread it over a piece of greaseproof paper and dry on a sunny windowsill or in a very low oven, once in a while using your fingertips or fork to break apart any nuggets.

- As a starting point, go with a herb to salt ratio of 2:1 by weight. Store in a sealed container as soon as you have dried the salt to retain that flavour.

- Single herb salts read clearly on the tongue, but don't let that stop you playing with combinations, such as lemon verbena and bay, orange thyme and fig leaf, or the marjoram and chive salt on page 104.

Herb sugars

As with salts, making herb sugar allows you to preserve a herb's flavour to enjoy another time, and there is a sweet intensity that the process captures that is different from adding them separately.

For sugars made with dried herbs, just mix with a similar quantity of sugar and allow the flavour to move into the crystals over a few days or weeks.

Mostly, I use fresh herbs to make sugars. When the herbs are your own or you are confident they don't need washing, swizz relatively equal quantities of sugar and leaves together in a coffee/spice grinder – the leaves' moisture creates a smoothish paste. In 15–20 minutes in a low oven it will happily dry into nuggets that can be swizzed into a gloriously intense powder.

With herbs that need washing, it is often impractical to get the leaves dry, so having shaken and kitchen-papered off as much of the water as I can, I swizz in the grinder in the same way, to form a wetter paste, one I find takes so long to dehydrate in the oven that it loses at least some of its flavour profile, so I leave it as a paste.

Herb butters

The anchovy butter in my last book, *Sour* (it's worth buying for this alone, tightwads), is a favourite, but I'm rarely without a few herb butters on the go. You can make them at the time you need them but being able to pull out a ready-made baton from the freezer to slice fat coins from is just great.

About 80g (3oz) butter is a good default quantity, that, as a rule of thumb, I'd suggest matching with 30 per cent the weight of the herb. If in doubt, go large with the herb.

There are two types of herb butter: the simple butter-and-herbs kind, and that where more ingredients are involved.

The approach I take most often is the former; of working leaves (stripped from the stem and finely chopped if required) into butter with my fingers until well incorporated: the resulting butter is ideal for pushing under chicken skin or finishing a steak. The other method is for incorporating ingredients that are either liquids or in small amounts (garlic, lemon zest, chilli flakes, etc.) that are harder to work consistently through the butter: these I make in double quantities, using a stick blender or small food processor.

I rarely add liquids as it's a nuisance to blend, and I find lime or lemon zest adds more of what I want than either juice. A finely chopped shallot, garlic minced to a cream, chilli flakes, black pepper and citrus zest are the additions I find work best in herb butters. Of course, prove me wrong with lime juice or whatever you fancy.

You can store the butter in a small plastic tub, but I prefer rolling it into a semi-formed baton and wrapping in greaseproof paper to roll more perfectly, twisting the ends to create a sliceable cylinder.

Herb jellies

I find herb jellies similar to marmalade; I don't want them that often but when I do, I *really* do. The principles are simple: apples (or similar) are cooked in combination with your chosen herb(s), a little acidity by way of vinegar or lemon and a good deal of sugar. The set result makes an excellent accompaniment to salty or fatty meats, cheese (especially blue) and as part of a gravy.

The core method I use is a sort of hybrid of my preserving-queen friend Pam Corbin's recipe and a few tweaks that experience tells me suit my taste. It is sweet but not crazily so, and I think this allows the purity of the herbs to shine. Adding the herbs in two stages brings brightness from the late herbs, and depth from the early. The choice of acidity is yours: vinegar gives a bold sourness against the sweet, whereas citrus juice does so a little more lightly; both are excellent.

This is a two-stage process that uses little of your time, but has an overnight spell for the juice to drip through. Ahead of the second stage, chill a couple of small plates or saucers and sterilize your jars on a hot dishwasher cycle (see overleaf).

A few suggestions for alternatives you may wish to try are also included, below. This makes 1kg (2lb 4oz) of jelly.

Ingredients

1kg (2lb 4oz) cooking apples

1 unwaxed lemon, roughly chopped

1 litre (1¾ pints) water

50g (2oz) herbs (approx), leaves stripped from the stems

670g (1lb 7oz) sugar (approx)

100ml (3½fl oz) vinegar or lemon juice

Very briefly swizz the unpeeled, uncored apples in a food processor until smallish and place in a good-sized pan with the lemon and water. Bring to a simmer and cook, covered, for 15 minutes. Stir occasionally, but avoid mashing the fruit. Add the herb stems and half of the leaves and cook for another 10 minutes or so until the apples are soft.

Pour boiling water over a jelly bag or muslin-lined fine sieve to sterilize it and set this over a large bowl. Tip the appley pulp into the bag/sieve and allow it to drip through for a few hours, ideally overnight. You have a choice here: you can hurry this along by squeezing the bag/muslin, but this will likely result in a cloudy jelly. If a cloudy (though no less delicious) jelly is the least of your worries, squeeze away.

Pour into a jug or bowl so that you can accurately measure (digital scales are often ideal) the volume of apple stock; discard any sediment that may have settled at the bottom of the bowl the apples were draining into overnight. For every 100ml (3½fl oz) of liquid you will need 65g (2½oz) sugar.

Pour the appley stock and the sugar into a large pan – ideally a preserving pan – and bring to a simmer, stirring frequently to dissolve the sugar. Add the vinegar or lemon juice and bring to a rolling boil. After 8 minutes, you can start testing for the setting point, i.e. when the jelly is ready to jar. Add a few drops to a chilled saucer and after a minute push it with your finger: if it wrinkles on the surface, it has reached the setting point; if not, boil for another 3 minutes and try again, repeating if necessary, until the drops wrinkle on a cold saucer.

Remove from the heat and stir with some enthusiasm to incorporate the scum, skimming off any that stubbornly remains. Chop the remaining herbs and add them, then allow the jelly to cool for 5–10 minutes; this allows the herbs to take in moisture and makes it less likely that they will rise to the surface when poured into jars.

Pour into sterilized jars, securing the lids immediately. If the herbs start to rise, invert the jars for a few minutes after half an hour or so and this should spread them through the jelly as it thickens.

Variations
Mojito jelly: use lime juice instead of vinegar and a bright variety of mint, ideally Moroccan mint.

Quince: using grated, unpeeled quince instead of or as part of the mix with apples works really well, as does using some blackberries: the weight of fruit is the crucial constant you need to maintain.

Combinations

So often a single herb is the perfect symphony. A tangle of mint in a cold, tall glass, a confetti of coriander over aloo chaat or half a Christmas tree of rosemary in with the lamb is the single note that creates harmony or satisfying discord. Simplicity is so often the answer.

Sometimes, however, the magic is created with a little interplay between herbs. The potential for combinations is almost limitless, and while jumping enthusiastically into the lake is to be encouraged, there are a few jetties that over the decades have shown themselves to be worthy of consideration. These range from simple, exquisite pairings such as lemon verbena and mint, to dry blends with centuries of use to recommend them such as herbes de Provence, to the addition of acids, fats, spices and more to create rubs, sauces and dips that can transform what you eat.

Many sauces and other combinations are close relatives: gremolata – a joyous blend of garlic, salt, lemon zest and (usually) parsley – is really not so very different to (say) salmoriglio sauce, where those flavours are carried in a sea of lemon juice and olive oil. A sense of those connections, and an appreciation that fats and acids help get the best from herbs will transform your cooking. As well as being wonderful in themselves, I hope those recipes are confidence-givers, dot-joiners and shortcuts to what will elevate this or luxuriate that. Make them as they are, to get a feel for them, but please remember not to be chained to the recipe: they are all jump-off spots into the lake, it is up to you how you swim.

INFUSING

Much of the time, it is not the herb itself we want to eat but its ghost. Bay is as palatable in the mouth as the wrapper of a dishwasher tablet, but – as with many things – a little warmth will tease a great deal out of a situation that coldness won't. Let a few bay leaves sit in warm oil, water or dairy and it gives you all it has to give. Try the bay liqueur, the bay chocolate cake, the onion tart, and bay in place of lemon verbena in the rice pudding recipe, and you'll see how differently influential it can be when infused, and yet somehow remain very much itself.

The same is true of fig, blackcurrant, lemon verbena, pandan leaves and many more. Even softer herbs can take to infusions well: tarragon lets go so much of what makes it special in sugar syrup, and lemon thyme infused into milk to become custard makes for a really special trifle. The possibilities and combinations of infusions are almost without end and, frankly, when most of them can be bent into a cocktail or two, there is quite the incentive for pleasurable experimentation.

Dairy infusions
Flavour falls into dairy like rain into midsummer soil. Milk and cream seem to have spaces left in their molecules awaiting exactly the sorts of flavours that herbs carry. Whether soft or woody, perennial or annual, subtle or bold, herbs just want to give themselves to the milkiness.

There are a good few dairy infusions in this book – from the semi-firmness of the fig leaf custard in the trifle on page 245, to the rice pudding on page 229, to the ice creams on page 235. While delicious in themselves, each sets the imagination ticking on other possibilities. In general, nothing more boisterous than warming and a bare simmer is needed.

Of course, non-dairy milks and creams can work perfectly well in place of animal dairies, though each has its own characteristics and the recipe may need a little tweaking. I have used oat milk (the creamier sort, sold as a partner for coffee) for each of the recipes and they have all worked well.

Herb syrups
These are the infusions I make most. If ever I have herbs in danger of going over, or plants in need of a trim, a syrup is their likeliest destination. Lemon verbena, ginger rosemary, blackcurrant sage, lemon thyme, scented geranium and bay are particular favourites, though my current belle is tarragon syrup.

As the later pages illustrate, I tend to use herb syrups in cocktails, but they lend themselves well to drizzling over cakes as you traditionally would lemon syrup, for pouring over pancakes and waffles, and the syrup infusion process is at the heart of a whole world of sorbets and granitas, including those on pages 238–9.

Woody herbs tend to be best. There is no need to be too prescriptive about the amount to be added: a handful to 500g (1lb 2oz) syrup is good; remove the herbs when the syrup tastes as you would like. Obviously, it'll be a little longer if you add less of the herb and vice versa.

The method is simple: place an equal weight of sugar and water (500g/1lb 2oz of each is good) in a good-sized pan, stirring as it warms to dissolve the sugar. Once at a simmer, remove from the heat and add the herb. Taste after a few minutes, removing the leaves when the syrup is as you would like. Depending on the herb and the quantity used, this may be a few minutes or half an hour. Strain into a sterilized bottle and refrigerate. Syrups will keep for weeks, often months, in the fridge.

Herb vinegars

The trickiest part of making herb vinegars is choosing the right herb(s) and the best vinegar for them; the process is reassuringly unmess-up-able.

Some principles:

- Avoid using anything metal in the making or storing. Rubber-sealed glass jars are ideal.

- Lightly bruise the herbs with a mortar and pestle or similar before using. The first word of that sentence is crucial; we are not making pesto until page 98. Loosely fill a sterilized jar with the leaves and cover with vinegar, ensuring the leaves are below the surface.

- I usually use white wine vinegar or cider vinegar; occasionally red wine vinegar with rosemary or one of the other woody herbs. Use good-quality vinegar of a minimum 5 per cent acidity (it should be written on the label); it doesn't have to be crazily expensive but ascending the quality ladder will affect the results. If you are not planning on keeping the vinegar long, you can ease the acidity back with a little water if it suits.

- Allow the herb to infuse in the vinegar in a dark place for a fortnight minimum; ideally a month. At this point, decant into a bottle, straining out the herbs, which you can use for cooking or discard. The vinegar will keep indefinitely, though the character often loses brightness but gains depth.

- I find small batches – a litre (2 pints) or less – are best. It's often tempting to make a big batch as the increased palaver of making more is incrementally small – but resist unless you are knocking up presents before Christmas; it's much more pleasurable to use a selection of vinegars at their peak than work your way through litres of just one.

Herb oils

Herb oils require a little patience to make well, but the method is simple and the same whatever the herb. I almost always use olive oil, though light alternatives such as avocado oil and sunflower are worth trying.

Blanch quickly in simmering water for 5–10 seconds to enliven the herb's essential oils and remove any potential for unhelpful bacterial activity, then plunge into cold water, drain and squeeze/pat the leaves dry.

Purée the leaves in a blender on high with the oil, and strain through a double layer of muslin. The more thorough the straining, the more glowing the oil, with less cloudiness. You may be moved to strain twice for a clearer oil. Or you may not.

This works equally well with woody herbs as it does the soft summer herbs such as coriander and basil. My favourites are tarragon (young leaves tend to be sweeter), basil, lemon thyme and summer savory.

Small batches are sensible as the flavour of herb oils tends to slide after a fortnight or so.

Of course, you can – as I often do – make a quick unstrained version that's something of a halfway house between a 'proper' oil and a pistou. Either way, I'd suggest freezing any you aren't going to use within a few days as this preserves much of its excellence.

If you are looking for a quicker result, by all means pour pan-warmed oil over a bowl of herbs (woody herbs are by some distance the best here) and allow its warmth to draw out the leaves' flavour as it cools. Strain or pick out the leaves and bottle the oil.

Both methods suit the clarity of a single herb, though there's one exception I make often: the tarragon and parsley oil on page 117.

These oils are also the first step on the spectrum into oily sauces and a whole world of dressings.

Muddling

How you treat herbs in a cocktail greatly influences the pleasure in the drink. Gentleness is important. Muddling is the art of encouraging the scent and flavour from leaves (or fruit) without producing bitterness or mush. Muddling implements are available to buy, but I use the handle of a wooden spoon.

Gently press the leaves against the base of a glass with a gentle twisting motion: the idea is to agitate the herbs thoroughly enough to release flavour and scent without puréeing them.

The rewards of doing this well are most perfectly demonstrated in making a mojito, where encouraging the oils from the lime and the mint transforms the cocktail from good to proper Cuban.

HERBS TO GROW AND EAT

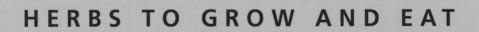

THE BOUNCER AT THE DOOR

As easy as it is to enthuse wildly in these pages, it's equally difficult to decide what to omit. I've applied all sorts of rules for myself, each irregularly and illogically broken. This is a personal selection, with all the bias, contradiction and inconsistency that that implies. I've focused on leaves – allowing seeds (such as those of fennel) to fall into a box labelled Spices, leaving out horseradish and garlic as they just don't feel like herbs as much as wildly poky entities that are some delightful halfway house between herbs, wet spices and vegetables.

I've included leaves not generally thought of as herbs – those of the fig and blackcurrant, for example – that work in similar ways to bay. Others have slipped past the troll on the bridge simply by being occasionally excellent, and if I've mentioned some herbs only briefly it is not intended to besmirch their fine name, but to reflect their infrequent but much-enjoyed appearance in my kitchen.

Angelica, for one, is utterly beautiful and a pleasure to have in the garden, but really – I use it for candying or to go with rhubarb less frequently than The Blue Nile release an album. A couple have been left out for other reasons: lemon balm is for people who dislike themselves enough not to grow lemon verbena; celery leaf and par-cel (both differently between parsley and celery) are perfectly good, but their uses are largely covered by lovage and parsley, so by all means play with both with that in mind.

There are others that sit on the fuzzy edge between vegetable, edible flower, salad leaf and herb. I might have quite reasonably followed other authors by including marigolds, rocket, rose and a whole world of alliums (such as Welsh onion) that are no more than a hair's breadth along the evolutionary spectrum from the chives that have made these pages. But I didn't.

The following pages aim to give you all you need to get the best from each herb on the entire journey from plot to plate. They include how to grow each herb, so I've omitted some herbs from the main list that feature in the book if they are almost always bought rather than grown (e.g. avocado leaves) or foraged (e.g. wild garlic).

I've kept winter and summer savories together as their culinary affinities are so similar; oregano and marjoram may be similar horticulturally, but my appetite thinks of them as distinct and I use them largely with different partners. Anise hyssop and Korean mint share the spotlight as they are so similar visually, and the heart of their sweet aniseed/mint scent and flavour is shared, yet one leans towards mint and the other to aniseed.

Some – and I'm thinking particularly here of Vietnamese coriander and pineapple sage – might well claim a spot of their own in this section as I love both so, but they fall onto the Other Favourites pages, largely thanks to the relatively narrow culinary range in which I use them. This should not be read as a comment on their excellence: I would not be without any of them.

There may be other ways to grow some of these herbs, and there may be affinities that you prefer; this is what I do and those that I like. Feel free to do as you fancy.

ANISE HYSSOP AND KOREAN MINT

Anise hyssop
Agastache foeniculum

Herbaceous perennial

✂ Mid spring to the start of autumn

1m (3ft) tall, 30cm (12in) wide

Korean mint
Agastache rugosa

Herbaceous perennial

✂ Mid spring to the start autumn

1m (3ft) tall, 30cm (12in) wide

Affinities

Chicken
Seafood
Fish
Eggs
Cheese
Asparagus
Beetroot (beet)
Carrots
Courgettes (zucchini)
Cucumber
Green beans
Salad leaves
Sweet potatoes
Tomatoes
Apples
Apricots
Melon
Nectarines
Peaches
Pears
Strawberries
Sugar

Anise hyssop looks like the offspring of a one-night stand mint had with a nettle. Its flavour is of gentle, minty, sweet aniseed, as its other name – liquorice mint – suggests. Korean mint is clearly its sister in looks, scent and flavour, but anise hyssop leans towards aniseed and Korean mint towards the Extra Strongs. They share culinary affinities, but those distinct leanings have a different impact, with anise hyssop being warmer, and Korean mint bringing a fresh brightness that's more zippy. Both go beautifully with shellfish and stone fruit; they also make the garden somewhere I want to go.

The flowers of both are extraordinary; by the time hot weather arrives, each stem is set alight with a flowering purple flame that draws a rich diversity of pollinators. You may even see finches pecking at the seeds. Anise hyssop is native to the prairies of North America, and it was also widely planted there in the nineteenth century so that bees might produce anise honey; you can mimic that combination, using either herb, by infusing the leaves or flowers in warm honey. The shades of purple in the flowers and green in the leaves are so tasteful you might choose them as paints. For so many reasons, these are two of my favourite herbs.

How to grow

Start with a young plant, or sow seed in spring, in modules and under cover (it needs warmth and light to germinate), barely covering with compost. Plant out after the last frost. Sow direct into a nicely prepared soil from mid spring and hope for good weather. A sunny spot in a rich soil is ideal.

Cut back to 5cm (2in) above ground when flowering to encourage new leaves – in truth, I only do this with a small patch; the flowers are so special, as well as being as delicious as the leaves. Once the flowers go over, cut back to encourage more to follow. Don't be surprised when they die back in winter; you'll see them again in spring. Will self-seed if allowed.

Harvesting

Pick leaves, flowers and seeds as you want them: I tend to pinch out the tops early on to encourage the plant to bush out, and later take leaves from the sides as I want flowers to come.

When/how to use

Neither like heat, so add leaves late, uncooked. Try it anywhere you like mint. The leaves and flowers are very good infused, either in sugar syrup, honey or vinegar, and they make an excellent herb sugar. And, as one who isn't a herbal tea fan, they make one of the finest.

BASIL

Ocimum basilicum

Half-hardy annual

✂ Late spring to early autumn

60cm (24in) tall, 50cm (20in) wide

Affinities

Chicken

Cheese, especially mozzarella, feta, halloumi

Eggs

Aubergines (eggplant)

Avocado

Courgettes (zucchini)

Cucumber

Garlic

Green beans

Peas

Potatoes

Sweetcorn

Tomatoes

Blueberries

Lemon

Raspberries

Strawberries

Stone fruit

Nuts

Lemongrass

Makrut lime

Basil is the scent of a summer spent somewhere you're not. It pairs beautifully with tomatoes and other summer vegetables, but only when they are exquisite: it refuses to cheer up the bland. I use it less frequently than most – like 'Mr Blue Sky', it appears too often when the sun's out, making me wish for autumn – but as with mint, growing your own basil allows you to explore different varieties, everything from lime basil to cinnamon basil. Its flavour and scent – which vary considerably according to variety – is a peculiarly appealing coming together of aniseed, menthol, ginger and more. Explore widely.

Varieties

Like cousins at a family wedding, the differences between basil relatives can be striking. Sweet Genovese is perhaps the best of the familiar basils, with lemon basil an excellent variation. I use the tiny-leaved Greek basil (*Ocimum minimum* 'Greek') most.

Thai basil (*Ocimum basilicum* var. *thyrsiflora*) has very mild mint, liquorice and nutmeg notes alongside the familiar basil, that give the leaves – certainly when homegrown – a scent that's similar to cardamom leaves. It is widely used in Vietnamese and Thai cuisine.

Holy basil, aka tulsi, is a different species (*Ocimum tenuiflorum*) to familiar basil, and has a spicy, clovey flavour. It is used throughout Asia, especially in Thai cooking, and is highly valued in Hindu culture as the leaves were used to scent temple water and believed to enable the soul to ascend to heaven.

How to grow

Basil loves warmth. Sow into modules or small pots under cover in spring, covering with a thin layer of vermiculite. Use a propagator or cover the pot with a freezer bag to up the temperature; once germinated, remove the covering. When they've developed their first true leaves, plant into 9cm (3½in) pots, then into their final location when you feel comfortable drinking an evening G&T in a T-shirt in the garden. Water the compost (not the leaves) regularly, in the morning: basil hates having wet feet overnight. Cut back to encourage new leaves to form, or enjoy the delicious flowers.

Harvesting

Pick leaves from the top of the plant to encourage new growth and a bushier shape. Take care – they bruise easily. Put cut lengths in a glass of water to extend their life. Don't refrigerate; this accelerates their decline.

When/how to use

Basil's flavour floats away in the steam of any heat, so it's almost always best added on serving. The exception is if gently warmed in milk, cream or oil to extract the flavour. Thinly sliced basil in salads of all kinds and scattered over pasta dishes, brings both depth and lightness. Perhaps its greatest quality is taking so well to sauces and oils – pesto, salsa verde and others. Basil dries unusually well for an annual herb. It also retains its flavour well if frozen in a purée (page 106).

BAY

Laurus nobilis

Evergreen perennial

✄ Year round

Can grow to a few
metres if allowed

Affinities

Almost everything,
but especially:

Lamb

Fish

Milk

Cream

Lentils

Tomatoes

Citrus

Poaching pears, peaches
and other stone fruit

Sugar

Most herbs

Vodka

Fresh bay leaves are a sweet coming together of summer and autumn, with
hints of citrus, rose, Pepsi, cardamom, nutmeg, vanilla and – depending on
the degree of drying it may have undertaken – lemon and pine. There can even
be a little smoky burning fruit wood in the background, reminding me of the
old streets of Winchester, in November. It somehow manages to be bold yet
gentle, with its warm, full spiciness.

Bay is perhaps the most versatile of herbs, working with so much savoury,
sour or sweet. It is a slow herb, releasing its flavour over time, in warmth, in
liquid. Don't eat the leaf itself; it is like crisp leather and peculiarly – given its
infused flavour – bitter in the mouth.

Varieties
Generic bay is the most widely available, but the flavour varies in intensity
between fresh and dried.

How to grow
Tricky to propagate, bay grows slowly when young. Save yourself the trouble
and buy a large plant.

Bay likes sun, a rich soil and shelter – if you are anywhere cold, grow it in a
pot until it's a few years old and woody enough to survive. Don't let it dry
out. Bay needs little ongoing care: a fortnightly feed through summer when it
is young is wise.

Harvesting
Pick as you need, all year round. Pluck leaves from the branch with a
downward motion rather than a cut; you don't want to snip the little bud at
the base from where a new leaf will spring. Pick mature leaves – they have
more flavour than the youngest.

When/how to use
Bay is one of the great infusers: its flavour travels slowly across its waxy
exterior – liquid is the passport. I particularly love bay infused in milk, white
sauces, rice pudding, custards and sugar syrups. It is rarely eaten, as such,
unless ground to a fine powder as a herb sugar or salt. Add early to soups,
stews and so on. You can push bay leaves into slits in roasting meat and fish,
where the cooking juices smuggle its flavour into the flesh. And if you are
making a curry or other dish where spices are fried early, add a bay leaf or
two. Bay branches are excellent on the barbecue, or in a smoker too. Twist
and crack, as the Beatles almost said, to encourage its flavour out.

Go easy when using dried leaves – while their flavour is weaker than fresh and
they can be excellent to use, they can leave a peculiar acrid flavour if too many
are employed.

Bay keeps for an age. In the fridge, in a sealed bag or Tupperware, no flavour
is lost. Discard dried leaves after 9 months as they become a ghost of
themselves. Bay salt (page 28) is superb, and you must try Allorino (page 258).

CHERVIL

Anthriscus cerefolium

Hardy annual

✂ Year round

30cm (12in) tall, often shorter

Affinities

Chicken

Crab, lobster, scallops, oysters

Dairy, especially sour cream, butter and soft cheese

Eggs

Lentils

Asparagus

Beetroot (beet)

Broad beans

Carrots

Celeriac

Courgettes (zucchini)

Green beans

Leafy salads

Peas

Potatoes

Tomatoes

Mushrooms

Chervil is a subtle yet beautifully present herb; it's not about to overpower anyone, even if generously deployed, so use it like it's Christmas. Delicate both physically and in flavour, chervil's leaves look like a lacier version of coriander, with a flavour that's a gentle halfway house between parsley and tarragon: sweet, bright and grassy, with a backbeat of aniseed. Chervil is – as herbs with aniseed often are – a great catalyser, making other herbs taste more of themselves when used in combination. If you don't have it, a combination of parsley and tarragon does a passable impression, lessening the amount that you'd use if adding chervil.

Varieties
Widely available as generic chervil, though there is, like parsley, a curled version.

How to grow
Easy from seed: sow direct from early spring until late summer, 1cm (½in) deep with 10cm (4in) between seeds. A rich, moist but well drained soil in half-shade is ideal as too much sun or too little water will encourage it to bolt. Be generous: you'll want to use it. It can take three weeks to germinate. Chervil is short-lived: sow monthly for a constant supply. Cut off the flower stems to extend its life. It can be grown through the winter in a very sheltered or undercover spot. Self-seeds merrily.

Harvesting
Ready to harvest in 6–10 weeks. Harvest outer leaves, leaving two-thirds unpicked to provide the engine room for more to grow.

When/how to use
Chervil's flavour is lost to too much heat: add it on serving to retain its subtle flavour, or add late to omelettes and soups. Be generous.

Chervil loves butter: try it with new potatoes, buttery scrambled eggs, or with the smallest of excellent carrots. Chervil butter (page 30), made with salt, black pepper and a little lemon zest, should be in every freezer to call on when you want. Chervil is frequently found in classic French dishes, often with tarragon, chives and parsley in the fines herbes mix used in omelettes and creamy sauces.

Chervil keeps only for a few days in the fridge.

CHIVES

Allium schoenoprasum

Hardy perennial

✂ Spring to autumn, with a little over winter

40cm (16in) tall

Affinities

Rice

Beef

Ham

Chicken

Smoked fish

Butter

Cream

Soft cheese

Eggs

Avocado

Carrots

Courgettes (zucchini)

Potatoes

Tomatoes

Most soft herbs

Vinegar

The tall, thin tubular leaves of chives grow in tight clusters that once in flower look like a clutch of purple sparklers. The flavour of leaf and flower is beautifully oniony – somewhat full-on without being harsh. I use the flowers more than the leaves – to me they are the main harvest, casting bright punctuation through salads, over the top of burgers and so on. Chives are widely available in supermarkets, but are so much better grown yourself as their intensity fades quickly after harvesting – more so on chilling.

Varieties

Purple- and white-flowered are the two main options; they taste the same, so choose for looks. Garlic chives are a wonderful twist on the familiar that, with their thicker garlicky stems, can take just a little more cooking.

How to grow

One for the terminally incompetent, chives will grow almost anywhere, but give them a rich, moist but well-drained soil and they will thrive. Start with a plant or two and grow where it's easy to harvest as they'll be there a long time. A liquid feed once in a while will keep them gloriously productive. Divide clumps to refresh and multiply your plants (page 18). Many close relatives – including Welsh onions – are well worth exploring too. You will be advised to cut them back to 3cm (1¼in) to encourage new leaves to grow – and this is perfectly sensible – but it will deprive you of the extraordinary flowers; grow some for leaves, some for flowers.

Harvesting

Harvest as you need, cutting them close to the ground rather than the tips to avoid creating yellowy ends. Growth slows over winter, picking up with the first hint of spring. Expect flowers before the weather has really warmed up too. Don't use the flower stems: they're tougher than a teddy boy's drainpipes.

When/how to use

Chives are present enough not to get lost in the company of other strong flavours, which makes them ideal where you want to create a big, herby impression. Always add them towards the end of cooking, either to finish a sauce or to serve, as heat steals the flavour and replaces their taut chopped tubes with a slippery slime.

Ponytail the leaves and thinly slice, creating mini quoits to scatter the flavour widely. Break the flowers into tiny goblet-shaped florets to scatter on soups, leafy salads and when anything from fish to stews needs a good oniony punch. Chives love butter and cream, and are very good in a sandwich. Jerry Traunfeld wrote in his excellent *The Herbfarm Cookbook* of using more robust chive leaves – quickly blanched – as edible string to 'tie up a little bundle of green beans, secure a crêpe that's been gathered into a beggar's purse, or fasten a herb leaf that's bundled around a little piece of fish'.

You really have to make chive flower vinegar (page 122) – it looks and tastes even better than you'd hope.

CORIANDER

Coriandrum sativum

Hardy annual

✂ Spring to autumn, with a little over winter

50cm (20in) tall

Affinities

Chicken

Lamb

Pork

Fish

Seafood

Rice

Chickpeas (garbanzos)

Avocado

Carrots

Chilli

Courgettes (zucchini)

Cucumber

Garlic

Potatoes

Sweetcorn

Tomatoes

Lemon

Lime

Mango

Orange

Watermelon

Coconut milk

Curry spices

Lemongrass

Mint

Parsley

Aka cilantro, aka the room divider: to some their desert island herb, to others a mouthful of soapy repellence. I am one who comes to worship. Coriander has a peculiarly distinctive flavour that's almost medicinal, oddly citrusy without being zesty, and while it calls to me loudly of the food of hot places I've yet to visit, it is somehow beautifully cool. This superb duality means coriander works with other cooling herbs such as mint and lemongrass, as well as with the bright heat of chilli and ginger. It is perhaps the most global of all the culinary herbs, as at home in Mexican food as it is in Indian or Korean.

Varieties
Most varieties are indistinguishable in flavour ('Lemon' is a fine exception) but some such as 'Leisure' are slower to bolt (run to seed).

How to grow
Easy and quick to grow from seed in a sunny, fertile, well-drained yet moist spot. Sow direct – thinly – in spring and autumn (the cool slows its tendency to bolt), or in trays for micros, or in pots. Lightly cover with compost. Germination takes 1–3 weeks. With a little protection such as a cloche or in a polytunnel, you can pick into winter from an autumn sowing.

Ask any gardener and they will tell you that coriander bolts more quickly than any plant: pop down to the corner for a Mr Whippy and the coriander you planned on cutting for supper a few minutes before will be a leggy mess by the time you've finished the flake: sow every 3–4 weeks for a constant supply. Ensure the soil/compost is damp, but avoid overwatering. Containers should be 15cm (6in) deep as coriander is deep-rooting.

Harvesting
Cut 3cm (1¼in) above the ground, leaving at least 60 per cent of the plant as the engine room for more to grow. For seeds or flowers – and you may get them whether you want them or not – leave the plant unharvested in sunny weather; pick them when they are ready, hanging long stems upside down in a paper bag to collect the seeds as they dry. Being of the same family as carrot, you won't be surprised to know that the roots are delicious. Pick regularly once established to reduce the chances of bolting. The leaves store only for a week or so in the fridge.

When/how to use
Add late as coriander's flavour is strong but easily lost. The stems are full of superb flavour: all but the toughest can be used with the leaves if chopped finely. I often add them to cooked onions in the base of a soup; it broadens the flavour, creating complexity alongside the zing of leaves added on serving.

Coriander forms happy alliances with almost anything – fish, veg, meat – with one exception: coriander has an untidy arm wrestle with most woody herbs which neither side wins but both are diminished by.

Wash, but also pat thoroughly dry, as wet coriander leaves stick together like layers of slate.

DILL

Anethum graveolens
Hardy annual
✂ Spring to autumn,
with a little over winter
1m (3ft) tall

Affinities

Beef

Lamb

Fish, especially salmon and trout

Soft cheese and sour cream

Mayonnaise

Rice

Eggs

Avocado

Beetroot (beet)

Broad (fava) beans

Carrots

Courgettes (zucchini)

Cucumber

Gherkins

Horseradish

Onions

Peas

Potatoes

Capers

Lemon

Chervil

Chives

Lovage

Mint

I used to think of dill as I do Peter Cushing: cast in a few specific roles, for which only it will do. In recent years, I have come around to using it more widely, but it should be used thoughtfully, as it is a touch peculiar in flavour and scent: a combination of caraway, parsley and citrus rind that has something of the toilet cleaner about it. Not that I am averse to toilet cleaner, just not in my dinner.

Its close botanical relationship with parsley is not apparent visually – dill is tall, with ferny foliage, not unlike fennel: the leaves look more like the skeleton than the leaves themselves – but parsley is definitely sitting there in the flavour.

Dill's edible yellow flowers grow in inverted chandeliers; landing pads for a wide array of insects. The leaves are widely available to buy and the flavour not such a homegrown upgrade, so if you are short of space, give it to another herb.

Varieties
Generic but there are bolt-resistant varieties such as Tetra.

How to grow
Dill likes full sun, shelter from strong winds and a rich soil. Direct sow where you want to grow as it hates being transplanted. Allow 12cm (5in) between plants, pushing seeds 1cm (½in) below the surface and covering; sow more densely for mini versions. Sow every month or so between mid spring and late summer for a successional supply as it goes to seed readily. Water frequently to slow its drive to seed, unless it's seed you are after.

Harvesting
Once established, harvest the side branches and tops, cutting them close to the stem. Leaves harvested after flowering tend to be bitter, so keep the plant from bolting if leaves are your aim.

When/how to use
Dill is a bit of a Jessie when it comes to heat, yet is bold and robust enough to stand up to big flavours: oily and smoked fish, earthy vegetables, onions, vinegar and mustard won't cast it in shade.

Dill's characteristics suit pickles and cures. It must like the nature of preservation. It works well when pickling most vegetables, sharing a particular affinity with gherkins and cucumber. Famously, dill is a key ingredient in gravadlax (page 190).

There are days in early summer when all I want to eat is early, small, nutty potatoes in a mudslide of butter, mayonnaise, sour cream or a mustardy sauce (page 95): dill is almost always involved. Away from the heat of summer, I use it sparingly in leafy salads; perhaps the Scandinavian associations in my mind make me think of it as a cool weather leaf.

Don't over-chop: if it's cut too fine, dill's flavour doesn't read well on the tongue; it's like hearing a radio from down the corridor.

FENNEL

Foeniculum vulgare

Short-lived perennial

✂ Spring to autumn, with a little over winter

2m (6ft) tall

Affinities

Duck

Pork

Fish, especially oily types

Seafood

Cream

Feta

Eggs

Lentils

Rice

Beetroot (beet)

Courgettes (zucchini)

Cucumber

Potatoes

Tomatoes

Peaches and nectarines

Strawberries

This is the brother of bulb fennel – both *Foeniculum vulgare* – this one lanky, the other has the bigger arse; Laurel to the other's Hardy. Fennel is a beautiful tall plant, producing yellow umbels – clusters of upward-facing flowers – that continue the plant's visual similarity with dill. The distinctive aniseed flavour and scent of the wispy fronds are what I use most of – as a dash through salads and with fish, most usually. The seeds are also delicious and sold as the familiar spice.

Varieties

Bronze, purple and green varieties. The green is slightly the hardiest.

How to grow

While it supposedly prefers a moist, fertile soil, fennel germinates and self-seeds readily: throw some seed around and just you try and stop it. If you prefer, start fennel off in modules in spring, planting out when easy to handle. It seems to thrive even in poor, sandy soil, with attention. It can spread if the seed falls, so harvest the seed green as a bright spice. It may vanish through winter, and reappear in spring.

Harvesting

You can harvest fronds from when it emerges in spring, cutting side branches close to the main stems. The newest shoots tend to carry most flavour. Give them a shake to dislodge any sunbathing aphids.

When/how to use

The leaves' intensity of flavour tends to be fullest early in the season, with a sweetness and penetration of the aniseed that's not so apparent later, so bear this in mind with quantities.

Other than perhaps when stuffing a fish, I rarely use a lot of fennel: it has one of those intense flavours you can get too much of, when a gentle hand will keep you close friends. Mostly, a little here and there is where its magic works best: a few fronds in a leafy salad, or with fruit – it pairs beautifully with peaches and nectarines especially, and with pretty much any seafood. Fennel is a perfect example of how the nature of the chop makes a huge difference to its presence: a handful of inch-long fronds in a leafy salad bring bright punctuation, whereas the same amount finely chopped adds a background hum I find less satisfying. Where fine chopping works beautifully is as part of a dressing. As with dill, fennel's bright liveliness is very good in pickles.

In the spirit of public service, let me tell you that I allowed a handful of fronds to sit in a bottle of vodka for six weeks and while the result may not quite take you off to a sunny summer morning in Lille, it makes a fine Martini sundowner. In late summer into autumn, use the now-tougher stems and leaves as a bed for grilling or barbecuing fish and vegetables, as with the red mullet recipe on page 188. Dry the stalks for the smoker too.

FENUGREEK

Trigonella foenum-graecum

Annual

✄ Year round if grown under cover

30cm (12in) tall

Affinities

Lamb

Eggs

Chickpeas (garbanzos)

Lentils

Rice

Potatoes

Spinach

Curry spices

Mint

Also commonly known as methi, fenugreek is – like fennel – a herb that is perhaps most familiar in its seed form, as the basis for curries and other spicy dishes; the leaves are really worth getting to know. You should find fresh or dried leaves in specialist greengrocers or online, but fenugreek is also very easy to grow yourself. The flavour and scent are so evocative of my earlier experiences of curries here in Britain, so deeply transporting, that I am quite disposed to it for that alone.

Varieties
Generic.

How to grow
Fenugreek is best sown where you want to grow it, either into deep trays, pots or direct in the soil. Spring until mid summer is the best time. I usually scatter the seed aiming for around 4–5cm (1½–2in) spacing, give or take – a too-close neighbour can always be plucked and eaten once germinated. Cover seed in a few millimetres of compost. Germination is usually within a week or so, and growth encouragingly rapid. A well-drained soil in a sunny spot is ideal.

Harvesting
You could expect to pick fenugreek leaves between 4–8 weeks after sowing, depending on the time of year. You can let the leaves grow large but I tend to sow them fairly densely and harvest when small and repeat sow. Unless you are growing fenugreek for seeds, harvest the leaves before any flower buds start to form as the flavour diminishes from then on.

When/how to use
Fenugreek leaves are fairly mild when fresh, and used similarly to spinach, in combination with spices, potatoes, chickpeas and so on. Drying makes the leaves more bitter – in a good way – and brings a different tone to the fresh fenugreek leaf flavour. As with other herbs such as mint, it can be good adding dried leaves early in a dish – with the softening onions, even – and adding the fresh leaves late, to layer and develop the complexity of the flavours of the dish.

LAVENDER

Lavendula angustifolia

Hardy perennial

✂ Mid spring to the start of autumn

1m (3ft) tall and wide

Affinities

Lamb

Pheasant

Rabbit

Carrots

Celeriac

Ginger

Apples

Apricots

Blackberries

Blueberries

Cherries

Lemon

Plums

Rhubarb

Sugar

Honey

Pistachios

Rosemary

Much as I am unable to pass a football without inclining my foot towards it, I bend to every lavender plant and play the softest tug of war with its flowers to lend my hands its scent. Somehow its perfume matches its colour. It is, like New Order's 'Bizarre Love Triangle', as much uplifting as melancholic. With its dense silver-green core and purple, blue or white flowering satellites on long, thin stems, this perennial brings years of beauty and fragrance, providing structure through winter and drawing in the pollinators.

Varieties

Lavendula angustifolia is the best to cook with; other lavenders can be less sweet, a touch more medicinal, and can tend towards the fabric softener. *L. angustifolia* and its hybrids are also as hardy as any. I favour Munstead or Hidcote.

How to grow

Full sun, good air circulation and a well-drained spot are non-negotiables. Plant in mid spring as the soil warms. Pruning maintains health and prevents stragginess: snip back a little in spring when the leaf buds appear to remove frost damage and tidy the shape, and after the main dash of flowers in summer cut back to 3–4cm (1¼–1½in) below where the flower stems grew from. Don't cut into the woody parts as new growth rarely appears from these parts.

Harvesting

The young leaves are good, but the bold and clean flavour of the flowers just as they are thinking of opening is best. Cut from the base of the flower stem: they will keep in water or a bag in the fridge for a week.

When/how to use

Lavender shares enough of rosemary's deep, resinous pungency to work well on its own or paired with it when roasting lamb: try either chopped flower heads alongside, under or pushed into slits, as a marinade or a herb crust.

Lavender infuses beautifully. You can add chopped flowers into cake mixes or meringues, or as an infusion. A few dismembered flowers stuck to the buttered cake tin (as you might with lemon verbena leaves) is another fine way of instilling some of its flavour without actually eating any of the plant itself. Lavender sugar is fantastic to have around: swizz in a grinder to reduce the heads a little, then add sugar and blitz to incorporate. This is wonderful for shortbread or sprinkling on strawberries or when roasting apricots.

Lavender's sweet perfume and flavour complement earthy, bitter vegetables, such as celeriac (see Za'atar chicken with thyme butter and lavender celeriac 'dauph' on page 216). Try a few flowers in the water when boiling potatoes or carrots. Lavender vinegar is extraordinary, and a few drops on halved apricots or peaches before they roast brings even the most stubborn of unripe fruit alive.

Lavender dries well: hang long flower stems in good air circulation. The flowers should be fairly dry in 2–3 weeks: strip them from the stem and store in a sealed jar. The flavour will be less intense than when fresh, but superb nevertheless.

LEMONGRASS

Cymbopogon citratus

Tender perennial

✂ Year round

120cm (4ft) tall

Affinities

Chicken

Pork

Fish

Seafood

Rice

Chilli

Ginger

Garlic

Lemon

Lime

Stone fruit

Pears

Coriander (cilantro)

Lemon verbena

Mint

Coconut milk

Gin

Vodka

If you're not sure what a stick of lemongrass looks like, there'll be one in the fridge door, fossilized, beneath that disappointing goat's cheese. The stems are far from promising at first sniff, but – as with most of us – a little gentle encouragement from a rolling pin convinces it to give up its secrets. Its unique sweet, aromatic character is peculiarly pungent yet gentle, bright but with depth, and perfectly suited to sweet, savoury and anything in between. It is widely used throughout South East Asia and many will associate it most familiarly with Thai curries. It is a herb that rewards the curious; try it in rice pudding, and the limoncello recipe on page 262. Growing lemongrass gives you access to the leaves, with their flavour a milder version of the stem; superb especially in soups with carrot or squash.

Varieties
Generic.

How to grow
The warmer and sunnier its location, the more quickly productive and full-flavoured it will be. It is best in a container as it is hardy only to 7°C (45°F); outside in summer is fine, and indoors for the rest of the year.

Water daily, cutting back in the cooler months just often enough to keep the compost slightly damp. The ends of the leaves can turn brown; snip them off or nip back to the base. In autumn, cut back to 10cm (4in) from the base and stop harvesting; a flush of new growth will follow in spring. I tend to give them a liquid feed or two at this time. Repot in spring if needed.

Lemongrass is tricky and erratic from seed; buy a plant, or create your own from shop-bought lemongrass. Place a stem with a bit of base in a tall glass with a few inches of water in it, put in a sunny position and roots should quickly appear from the base. Pot the plant up and grow somewhere sunny. Over time, lemongrass forms clumps that can be divided to create more.

Harvesting
I tend to pick the stems when they are the thickness of a pencil and the leaves whenever I need them, from early summer into autumn.

When/how to use
The papery outer layer of lemongrass is just the envelope; within are the softer, lusher, wet layers that carry all that distinctive flavour. To release it, either place the stem on a chopping board and gently assault with a series of light rolling pin bashes along its length, or peel off the paperiness and slice thinly.

An essential in Thai curry pastes, but I find I'm constantly finding a new home for its distinctive floral lemoniness: the aforementioned limoncello; rice pudding is beautifully different with lemongrass in place of lemon verbena; and it's a pretty special part of the poaching for most fruit, but especially pears. A bashed stem added to cooking rice is a seriously good change.

If you are growing your own lemongrass, the leaves are wonderful in soups, on noodle dishes and in a refreshing tea, solo or with mint.

LEMON VERBENA

Aloysia triphylla

Half-hardy, deciduous perennial

✂ Mid spring to the start of autumn

Late spring to early autumn

Typically 1m (3ft) tall, 80cm (30in) wide; often much taller against a sunny wall

Affinities

Chicken

Duck

Fish

Dairy

Carrots

Courgettes (zucchini)

Apricots

Lemon

Peaches and nectarines

Pears

Rhubarb

Mint

Lemongrass

Sugar

Lemon verbena makes me happy. Were it toxic, I would love it for the days it leaves its scent on my fingertips. It is like lemons but better; full of sherbet and zest. It is everything lemon balm isn't. It is my desert island herb. Let us sow lemon balm for the pollinators and keep lemon verbena for ourselves. Keep it by the door, near where you like to lie when it's sunny, and perhaps have another on the sunniest windowsill. Too much is still too little.

The slender spearhead leaves are light green, eggshell in texture and finish, in triplets around the stem, emerging from early spring and hanging on until the first frosts – longer if sheltered. Tiny white flowers draw in the pollinators, and can be used in infusions along with the leaves.

Varieties
Generic only, though if you look widely you may find orange verbena too.

How to grow
Sunshine, shelter and a fertile, well-drained growing medium are essentials. Best in a container or, in milder latitudes, against a sunny wall so that it avoids winter's harshest attentions. Bring indoors for winter if you are in any less than a mild area, and water very sparingly then.

Pruning encourages the plant to become bushier; do this when spring is almost upon you, and in early summer. If you are after maximizing leaf production, remove the flower stems as you notice them.

Harvesting
Pick just above a pair of leaves as and when you need it.

When/how to use
As with bay, lemon verbena is not a leaf you want to eat whole. Grind it into sugars and salts (pages 30 and 28) and make superb infusions such as syrups, vinegars, custards and sorbets.

The fridge turns the leaves black, so any you aren't using quickly can be left on the windowsill to slowly desiccate – they'll retain most of their intensity for the next month or two. Store in a sealed jar to extend their life. Dried leaves can be reduced to dust in a coffee/spice grinder. Used fresh it will make a sugar paste; when dried it gives a bright dry sugar (or salt) to dust or ice whatever you choose. The paste freezes well, while remaining spoonable.

Lemon verbena also works really well as a magnifier with the sours as it has no sharpness of its own: add it when making lemon curd or ice cream to exaggerate the lemon without upping the sourness. It also makes one of the few really great herb teas; try a few leaves solo or with Moroccan mint.

Whole branches are so good for using on the barbecue, as skewers or in a smoker.

LOVAGE

Levisticum officinale

Hardy perennial

✂ March to October

2m (6ft) tall, 60cm (24in) wide

Affinities

Beef

Ham

Lamb

Seafood, especially mussels

Smoked fish

Pale, crumbly cheese

Eggs

Beans, especially borlottis

Carrots

Chard

Courgettes (zucchini)

Jerusalem artichokes

Onions

Potatoes

Spring greens

Swede (rutabaga)

Tomatoes

Apples

Parsley

Mushrooms

Vodka

Lovage is a beast. Take a strimmer to it and it returns like Monty Python's ailing knight: 'Tis but a scratch!' This is a plant you will never exhaust. You need a leaf or two at most yet, rich in irony, it grows tall as a ladder. The scent and flavour is a curious cross of celery and yeast; bitter, green and very savoury. It is as you'd imagine strong vegetable stock might taste in leaf form.

Scotch lovage is a smaller, waxy variety, slightly less intense in flavour. By early summer, it produces clutches of seeds that dance in the breeze like little fawn flies: their flavour is exactly like a newly creosoted fence smells. Unpromising, yes, but when have I ever lied to you: they are superb scattered in or on to a loaf before baking, and an excellent bottom end in a Bloody Mary.

Varieties

Familiar lovage and Scotch lovage.

How to grow

Lovage is easy: buy a plant and put it green end up, brown end down and you'll have a lifetime's supply. It is tolerant, but prefers deep, rich soil and part shade. Tame it once in a while, avoiding only the tender heart, composting what you don't need: catch it as the flower stems start to make a dash for it and new leaves will follow, or let it go and enjoy the seeds. Don't be alarmed when it dies back over winter – it'll be back in spring.

Harvesting

Pick leaves and seeds as you like from spring into autumn. The young leaves are most tender and best for eating raw; avoid the oldest as they can be very bitter. The stems are hollow – like soft bamboo; cut them back to stop them flowering if you like, but there are no shortage of leaves even with the plant's energies shared with flowering. The stems carry the same savoury flavour and make an excellent straw for a Bloody Mary.

When/how to use

Lovage's flavour is not dissimilar to celery and yet more like a really rich, intense vegetable stock. Use it where you want exactly that, but go easy – it has the depth of a woody herb in its soft, parsley-like leaves. Add it late for a bold impression, or early to allow its punch to soften a touch. In soups and stews that need widening out, lovage does an instant job.

Lovage accentuates leaves with a ghost of bitterness about them: spring greens and Brussels sprouts in particular. Its affinity with crisp apples makes a wonderful combination when cooking mussels in cider with just a couple of ribboned leaves of lovage. Try a lovage and apple sauce for pork, too.

You must try a pale crumbly cheese wrapped in lovage leaves (page 120). Lovage works peculiarly well with tomatoes: the thinnest slivers in place of mint or basil.

Lovage vodka (page 261) is marvellous, and apparently a little lovage works really well in whisky, but I'm not about to risk it on my Lagavulin.

MARJORAM

Origanum majorana

Tender perennial

✂ Summer into autumn

50cm (20in) tall

Affinities

Lamb

Fish

Cheese

Eggs

Beetroot (beet)

Carrots

Cauliflower

Courgettes (zucchini)

Potatoes

Squash

Sweetcorn

Tomatoes

Basil

Rosemary

Mushrooms

When I was 22, I went travelling about Europe. On the way to Turkey, the tiny ferry touched Crete as briefly as a fly nods a window, a handful of people stepping quickly on to the jetty and away. It was dawn, I'd slept on deck, and the scent as the morning air warmed the soil has never quite left my nose. I get a hint of it every time I rub the sun-warmed leaves of sweet marjoram, and for a millisecond I am 22.

Marjoram shares much with its very close relative oregano, and though less in your face it is no less characterful: it has bark rather than bite. Its flavour is of sweet, spicy pine plus citrus peel. I reach for it more than oregano, though there are times I want oregano's kick.

Varieties

There are a few with 'marjoram' in their name – Italian, French and Cypriot (each from other species) to name but three, and each can be good – but for me sweet marjoram is the best for the kitchen.

How to grow

Marjoram is a perennial in warm climates, but anywhere with a frost it's treated as an annual. You can start with plants or seed. Sow seed – mixed with sand to prevent oversowing as they are so fine – in pots from early spring and don't cover with compost; water and germinate in a propagator or airing cupboard. Then bring into the light and move seedlings into 9cm (3½in) pots to establish. Plant out when all danger of frost has gone. Give it a very well-drained soil and a sunny spot. The flowers are beautiful, full of that familiar scent and flavour, but they will slow the plant's leaf production down: prune it little and often for a long summer and autumn of harvesting. If you chop it back to 3cm (1¼in) in height, you might even get it to overwinter under cover.

Harvesting

Any time, but be aware that the intensity of scent and flavour increases considerably in hot weather and if grown in dryish conditions. Use strong scissors or secateurs to snip sprigs halfway down the stem.

When/how to use

Marjoram is a peculiarly under-appreciated herb. Oddly tropical, Mediterranean and everyday at the same time, it is wonderful in the summeriest dishes – such as barbecued sweetcorn – or enlivening something as autumnal as mushrooms fried in butter. Marjoram is very good in warm oil or butter – with spring greens, sweetcorn, over the nuttiest new potatoes and under the skin of chicken. As a rule, I add it towards the end of cooking – it can lose its flavour if thrown into a soup or stew too early.

As with thyme, strip leaves from the woodier cut stems (discard the latter), and chop the greener stems along with the leaves before using. The flowers are edible too, carrying a similar scent and flavour to the leaves.

MINT

Mentha spicata
Hardy perennial
✂ Spring into autumn
60cm–1.2m (2–4ft) tall

Affinities

Lamb
Tuna
Goat's cheese
Yoghurt
Rice
Bulgur wheat
Asparagus
Aubergines (eggplant)
Avocado
Courgettes (zucchini)
Cucumber
Garlic
Green beans
Peas
Potatoes
Tomatoes
Figs
Lemon
Lime
Mango
Melon
Peaches and nectarines
Pomegranates
Raspberries
Strawberries
Watermelon
Chocolate
Rum
Basil
Coriander (cilantro)
Lemon verbena
Parsley

There is really not much to beat lying in a patch of just-trimmed mint on a sunny day, when there is no one to observe your madness. To be consumed in that fragrance, that sea of freshness, is quite something. If you have a patch of lawn that you'd rather not mow, plant some mint and look forward to horizontal daydreams to come, otherwise grow mint in a container to curtail its spread. Along with lemon verbena, mint is perhaps the cheeriest of the herbs, and its numerous variations mean it is hard to tire of it.

Varieties
Mints are largely split into the spearmints (*Mentha spicata*) and peppermints (*Mentha piperita vulgaris*). The former have pointed (hence its name) leaves and a superb fruity coolness. Moroccan mint is one, and hard to beat. Peppermints tend to have rounder leaves, often darker in leaf and stem, with a serious coldness to the scent and flavour, as if they've been in the fridge. Moroccan mint, Chocolate/After Eight mint (exactly as you'd hope), Berries and Cream mint, Strawberry mint and Apple mint are all superb. There are varieties to avoid in the kitchen: Eau de cologne mint is like being hugged by that least favourite uncle, and Banana mint is like the worst service station banoffee pie eaten on a slow, rainy trip to a half term holiday with a car full of over-tireds.

How to grow
Mint is very hard to kill; it'll spring forth from the tiniest roots. Start from seed, or if impatient a young plant. Mint is very tolerant but prefers semi-shade, in a relatively well-drained spot that gets plenty of water.

Cut leaves back to encourage new growth. Allow mint to flower and the flavour and scent can turn from vital to vulgar; that said, the flowers are usually beautiful and much loved by insects.

Harvesting
Pick as you like; leaves will last up to a week in the fridge or in a glass of water. Dry by hanging upside down in a spot with good air circulation, then strip the leaves from the stem and store them in a sealed container.

When/how to use
Spearmints are the best for most recipes. Peppermint's full-on menthol-infused charge is too poky for most culinary uses, though occasionally perfect. Chocolate mint leaves in the poaching liquid for peaches is superb, and it makes an excellent bracing tea. Mint makes superb sugar syrups, and an excellent ice cream, where its 'cold' flavour suits perfectly.

All but the very smallest leaves tend to be too coarse to eat whole; reduce the rest to the thinnest of shreds. Muddling – agitating the leaves to release their flavour and fragrance – is ideal for drinks such as mojitos.

OREGANO

Origanum vulgare

Hardy perennial

✂ Year round

60cm (24in) tall

Affinities

Lamb

Tuna and other robust fish

Goat's cheese

Bread

Eggs

Aubergines (eggplant)

Cabbage

Courgettes (zucchini)

Squash

Sweetcorn

Tomatoes

Smoke

Mushrooms

Oregano and marjoram are horticulturally separated by a cigarette paper, but if you've ever had a life-saving rollie in a shop doorway when life has dealt you a cruel one, you know how important a cigarette paper can be. Oregano is marjoram's coarser brother, in a bolder, spicier, gimme-another-pint kind of a way. It sits somewhere between thyme, hyssop and sage in flavour, with crucial hints of mint and a pepperiness that stops just shy of chilli. I use it little, but when I want it – usually on something that gets cooked hot and hard, like pizza or griddled sweetcorn – there's nothing I'd rather have.

You may find shop-bought oregano to be milder than this sounds; you may even be unimpressed with the scent of a plant in a garden centre or nursery: if so, it is likely to be common oregano, or a hybrid thereof. Trust the scent it leaves on your hands and don't buy it if it's not lively. The flowers – a shower of small, pinky-white confetti – are as attractive to us as they are to beneficial insects.

Varieties

Hot and Spicy lives up to its name quite laughably: go easy with it. Greek oregano (O. *vulgare* subsp. *hirtum*) tends to be reliably distinctive and lively.

Oregano hybridizes so readily that the many names it can be sold under, some implying a country of origin, can be so variable: the only real guide is how you like the scent and flavour.

How to grow

Buy a plant that has the flavour you want, and then if you come to want more, propagate from cuttings (page 17) to ensure the same intensity of flavour and scent.

Give it a well-drained soil and plenty of sun. If growing more than one variety, keep them separate to avoid them blending. Over time, it can spread in conditions it favours, so grow it in a container if you'd rather it didn't.

Harvesting

Pick by cutting stems high or low, as you like. After flowering starts, you may want to cut the stems back hard, losing perhaps two-thirds to the secateurs, to encourage new leaves and give you plenty of cut stems to dry.

Oregano is superb dried: hang long stems upside down in a place with good air circulation for as long as it takes for the leaves to dry out completely: this can be a week or a month, depending on the time of year and the freshness of the leaves. Strip the leaves from the stems and store in an airtight container.

When/how to use

I find good oregano only sings loud, so is best in a noisy choir of garlic, chilli, pepper, anchovies, citrus and capers. Any combination drawn from that sun-loving ensemble works well, especially in tomato sauces, where olive oil is generously deployed and perhaps where smoke is involved in the cooking. Oregano is superb over flames or in the hottest of ovens: it stands its ground beautifully on pizzas, as barbecue skewers or in a smoker.

PARSLEY

Petroselinum crispum
Hardy biennial widely grown as an annual
✂ Year round
50cm (20in) tall

Affinities

Bacon/ham
Beef
Lamb
Fish
Seafood
Eggs
Lentils
Aubergines (eggplant)
Beans of all kinds
Courgettes (zucchini)
Carrots
Capers
Chilli
Garlic
Onions
Potatoes
Tomatoes
Winter root vegetables
Lemon
Nuts
Most other herbs
Mushrooms

It's a two-horse race between coriander or parsley for the herb I use most, and I love them equally, yet for something used so commonly and enthusiastically, parsley is strangely unremarkable. It doesn't have the wild zing of lemon verbena or even the peculiar medicinality of dill; it just complements and embellishes so very much in the kitchen, gently elevating without making a song and dance of it. Its flavour is distinctly savoury, very 'green' and a tiny bit bitter without ever going the whole lovage. I use it alone and with other herbs in sauces, salsas, pastes and so on as it has a beautifully generous habit of harmonizing with other herbs.

Curly parsley, with its crinkled leaves, has a slightly bolder flavour that is perfect when that's required – parsley sauce for one – but I tend towards flat-leaf for its softer texture and ease of chopping.

Varieties
Curly parsley (*P. crispum* var. *neapolitana*) and flat-leaved variations are your choice; the latter is sometimes sold as Italian parsley.

How to grow
Parsley is a biennial, largely grown as an annual as the leaves are much finer in year one. It is easy to grow from seed, from spring: it can take a month to germinate. It needs warmth and moisture to do so, and is best started indoors. It prefers sun with a little shade, a well-drained, rich soil and frequent watering. To grow it through winter, sow as summer eases into autumn.

Harvesting
Once established, harvest stems close to the ground, from the outside of the plant first. Leave half unharvested as the engine room for more leaves to follow.

When/how to use
Adding parsley late to a dish, and on serving, brightens it visually and in flavour; it will happily improve almost any savoury dish, meat, fish or vegetable. Its ability to enhance and embellish other herbs is one of the reasons I love it: it is part of the classic fines herbes blend (page 114), but it's good paired with any soft herb. Parsley pesto, parsley sauce, persillade and gremolata (pages 98, 131 and 112) are kitchen essentials.

Parsley makes a fine salad leaf: use the freshest leaves and dress it with a bright vinaigrette, alongside most fish, lentils or lamb chops.

Don't waste the stalks: add them early to soups and stews, and when making stock.

ROSEMARY

Rosmarinus officinalis

Hardy perennial

⊱< Year round

1m (3ft) high and wide, occasionally considerably larger

Affinities

Chicken

Lamb

Pork

Rabbit

Tuna, anchovy, bass and other oily fish

Goat's cheese

Bread

Aubergines (eggplant)

Beans

Carrots

Celeriac

Garlic

Olives

Onions

Parsnips

Potatoes

Squash

Sweet peppers

Tomatoes

Apples

Apricots

Grapes

Lemon

Orange

Peaches and nectarines

Plums

Rhubarb

Blackberries

Chocolate

Nuts, especially almonds

Mushrooms

Smoke

Gin

Piney-bright as rosemary smells on the fingers, it wakens to its full glory in ferocious heat. It is very lightly bitter yet sweet, resinous and deep while also uplifting – and it's not a misery guts the way sage can be. I've not roasted many potatoes or joints of lamb without its heavy presence. Native of the Mediterranean coast, you can assume it will enhance most of the foods synonymous with that area. Rosemary is one of the rare herbs where the flavour is so big, yet hard to overdo without really meaning to.

Varieties

There are many varieties of rosemary, some tall and slim – Miss Jessop's Upright for one; others prostrate and wide, and ideal for cascading over a wall or the side of a container. Ginger rosemary (sometimes sold as Green Ginger rosemary) is an absolute essential.

How to grow

Start with a plant, or propagated from cuttings. Give it the sun and the well drained soil its Mediterranean soul insists on. Despite rosemary's woody nature, it doesn't like a harsh winter; a well-drained soil, very occasional watering and shelter will do a lot to help it through the coldest months. Grow it against a warm, sunny wall or in a container where you can move it to a sheltered spot or under cover if your winters are harsh. Use a good potting compost for containers and feed it fortnightly or so through spring and summer.

Harvesting

Cut stems as you want them. Strip the leaves from the stem only if you are happy to allow the spikes to spread through the dish, rather than pull them out in one go by removing the branch. In winter, rosemary grows slowly, so harvest only a little. The flowers carry a sweeter version of that familiar flavour; try one, and you'll find every excuse to scatter them on salads and more.

Flavour and scent vary greatly in intensity with variety, time of year and temperature: trust your nose and tongue. You can always add a little more part way through the cooking if it's a slow-cook recipe.

When/how to use

Rosemary is very good to add early as it is robust both in physicality and flavour. Throw in when roasting potatoes, lamb and vegetables. The earliest softer leaves of spring are sweet and wonderful in a pasta sauce. As with so many of the oily, woody herbs, rosemary infuses beautifully in milk, cream, oil and sugar syrup. Add it to pizza and focaccia and it comes alive.

Rosemary makes a superb wood for the smoker, or cast on to hot charcoal or a wood fire to impart that characteristic flavour with the smoke; the main stems make fine skewers for the barbecue or oven.

That sweet piney flavour works well in some desserts: three of my favourites are very finely chopped in shortbread, used almost sparingly when poaching stone fruit and pears, and rosemary butter where the core used to be when baking apples.

SAGE

Salvia officinalis

Hardy perennial

✂ Year round

75cm (30in) tall and wide, occasionally more

Affinities

Chicken

Goose

Kidney

Liver

Pork

Salty meats such as bacon and prosciutto

Eggs

Blue cheese

Butter

Asparagus

Celeriac

Courgettes (zucchini)

Kale

Onions

Parsnips

Squash

Sweet peppers

Tomatoes

Apples

Grapefruit

Lemon

Pears

Pineapple

Most other woody herbs

Sage is the Roy Orbison of herbs: not something I want the company of every day, but when I do it's perfect. In the same way peppermint tastes cold, sage tastes dry. It has heft, earthy seriousness and an almost medicinal edge to its oily scent and flavour: it is in no way light-handed or anything, but very definitely savoury. The leaves are soft, leathery, and more pleasant on the fingers than on the tongue when raw, but cook them with something fatty like goose or – classically – pork, and it enriches in its low, deep way. It is happy in the extreme heat of a lively oven, barbecue or smoker. Homegrown sage is almost always more intense and complex than shop-bought leaves.

Varieties
Green sage is commonest and has the flavour I'm looking for most often, but there are variegated, purple, yellow and numerous other variations. As always, let flavour be your guide.

How to grow
Sage can be a little monkey to grow well, though many I know just pop a young plant in green side up and it flourishes; I hope you are one of the lucky ones. Full sun and a well-drained spot are crucial; if your soil is heavy, grow it in a container with a suitable peat-free compost and plenty of grit.

Cut back after flowering in spring, to half the length of the growth. Avoid pruning later in summer or autumn.

Harvesting
Cut single leaves or longer stems just above a pair of leaves. The scent and flavour varies wildly with time of year, temperature and exposure to sun, so use your judgment: if it smells intense, the flavour will be too. The flowers have a sweeter version of the leaves' flavour, but don't take any heat; pluck the petals from the calyx and add them to salads, poached pears, strawberries or over pasta.

Fresh leaves can keep for two weeks in a paper bag in the fridge. Sage dries really well hung upside down in inverted bouquets, or dried on a windowsill, before storing in a sealed jar.

When/how to use
Sage responds to slow cooking, giving up more of its complexity over time, as well as hot temperatures: try them fried quickly in butter and/or oil, where they become crisp, with the flavour mellowing a touch.

Sage was made for poultry and pork; that said, it pairs well with many vegetables, where its resinous medicinal melancholy seems made for the earthy, sweet roots and leaves of autumn especially.

Use sage semi-sparingly in poaching liquid for rhubarb or pears, in cakes (page 242) and try a few leaves warmed in honey to go with blueberries and pears.

Sage syrup is fine thing; the outstanding gimlet on page 264 will make you happy.

SALAD BURNET

Sanguisorba minor

Perennial

✂ Year round

80cm (30in) tall

Affinities

Fish

Ice cream

Soft cheese

Eggs

Broad (fava) beans

Potatoes

Tomatoes

White beans

Gin

Sugar syrup

Other soft herbs, especially parsley, chervil and tarragon

This tumbling mess of small, serrated-edged leaves straggles merrily all year round, with fresh lively leaves sprouting from spring into autumn. Its flavour is of clean, clear cucumber. I really don't use salad burnet in a hundred ways, but it is perfect to flavour water, occasionally in a gin and tonic and, as its name suggests, in leafy salads when its leaves are small and young.

Delicate as it appears, salad burnet overwinters well, but the thickened leaves of the cold months lack the brightness and supple texture to infuse or be chewed. I cut them back in spring to encourage new leaves. Little clusters of red/green flowers spring forth as the weather warms: I tend to leave them to beautify their corner, though they can hasten the leaves to toughen a little. If allowed, salad burnet will self-seed, blessing you with more plants the following year.

Varieties
Generic.

How to grow
Sow seed in small pots in mid spring, or buy a young plant and give it anything but a waterlogged or extremely sandy soil in which to grow, watering often as it establishes and through dry, hot spells. Cut back tough growth to encourage new leaves to emerge.

Harvesting
Pick all year round, but the young leaves in spring and summer have best flavour and texture.

When/how to use
I am fully aware that I have only scratched the surface when it comes to salad burnet: I use it most frequently in a few cocktails, adding it to water to go with a meal, in Pimm's and in salads, but I intend to use it to make a sorbet and ice cream to see if I can draw that bright coolness into them.

SAVORY — SUMMER AND WINTER

Summer savory (Satureja hortensis)

Hardy annual

✄ Mid summer to early autumn

50cm (20in) tall

Winter savory (Satureja montana)

Hardy perennial

✄ All year

40cm (16in) tall

Affinities

Beef

Lamb

Pork

Rabbit

Beans of all kinds

Beetroot (beet)

Brussels sprouts

Cabbage

Courgettes (zucchini)

Onions

Potatoes

Spring greens

Sweetcorn

Sweet peppers

Tomatoes

Winter root vegetables

Most woody herbs

Here, two plants that look and behave quite differently but share half a name and – more importantly – a deep, peppery, thymey savouriness. That flavour takes equally well to roasting with meats and vegetables, and works with both green beans, borlottis and other dried beans.

Winter savory is a bushy evergreen that can look like a football's been dropped in its guts; eager curled fingers pushing skywards at its edge, each producing small, dark green leaves all year round. If it could be bothered to get out of bed it'd easily reach 60cm (24in) tall. The creamy flowers in summer are quietly gorgeous. Summer savory is an annual, growing quickly to similar dimensions, in more of an indignant Christmas tree fashion. I love them both. The latter carries a less intense, less resinous flavour than winter savory which in turn has more sage and pine to it, like each was made by someone who knew what you wanted when. The joy of having both is that you can add peppery depth either early in slow-cooked dishes with winter savory, or late in little-cooked recipes using summer savory, or even use both to build complexity in soups, stews and so on.

Varieties
Widely available as winter and summer varieties, you might find Aromata (a poky summer savory), or Citriodora (a smaller, lemony winter savory).

How to grow
Sow summer savory in mid spring; a winter savory plant will have you in leaves almost immediately. Both prefer sun, a well-drained not-too-rich soil, and shouldn't be allowed to dry out. Prune summer savory back by two-thirds as it tries to flower to encourage more growth over a longer season; winter savory should be given a light trim just to freshen it up after it flowers, and dead and scrappy old growth cut back in early spring.

Harvesting
For both savories, cut stems around a third of the way down. Winter savory can be picked throughout winter but go easy, as it grows very slowly then.

When/how to use
As with most woody herbs, winter savory is fabulous when cooked long and slow in the liquid of a stew, or with cooking beans, whereas summer savory's softer texture makes it superb added to dishes later.

It's easy to think of the savories as just rosemary alternatives, but they deserve to be the subject of their own inquisitiveness. Summer savory on tomatoes, the smallest courgettes, in the presence of flames and smoke (try sweetcorn, lime, too much butter, salt, pepper and summer savory's piney excellence together) are fine places to start; either savory will thank you for cooking it like you hate it – hard and hot – in the presence of red meat, summer vegetables or green beans; and winter savory cosies up well with winter greens as well as cold weather roots. Winter savory is superb as a rub or marinade for meat, and either is fabulous in salami. Savory (either variety) is traditionally part of herbes de Provence, the classic blend of predominantly woody herbs.

SCENTED GERANIUMS

Pelargonium sp.

Tender perennial

✂ All year if under cover for winter, otherwise summer into autumn

60cm (24in) tall

Affinities

Dairy

Berries

Stone fruit

Honey

Sugar

For a long time, I had an aversion to geraniums of all kinds; they reminded me of where I grew up, pots commonly either side of the step up to the door for a splash of gaudy. Now, I love them for all those reasons, and for the perfume that the scented geraniums carry in their leaves.

From their South African origins, varieties have been developed with bold fragrance and flavour. The rose-scented variety is extraordinary: the leaves convey Turkish Delight flavour to warm milk, cream or sugar syrup. If you want to explore more widely, there are seemingly endless other variations to try: peppermint, orange, lime, lemon, hazelnut and pine among those I've grown in recent years. As with bay and blackcurrant leaves, you don't want to actually eat the leaves: they are tough and bitter.

Varieties

Attar of Roses is the classic, but you'll also find many other available, with new kinds constantly being raised.

How to grow

Scented pelargoniums are usually grown as annuals, though in a sheltered, warm spot against a house or other wall, or brought under cover for winter, they will survive and even be lightly productive during the cold months. They will thrive in any sheltered, sunny spot, indoors or out, with a well-drained, rich soil/compost. Feed every month during summer to keep them productive. If growing in containers, move up a size each autumn, adding fresh compost and cutting growth back by a third: it may pretend to be sulking for a while but it will re-emerge in early spring.

Harvesting

Pinch or cut off leaves as you need them, never more than one third of the plant at a time to allow it to recover.

When/how to use

The softly lobed, often slightly furry leaves are not to be eaten; infusing is the best means of extracting the flavour. Take the milk, cream or sugar syrup off the heat before adding the leaves, tasting frequently, before straining the leaves out when the intensity is as you'd like. Once captured, that flavour is ready for custards, jellies, ice creams, cakes, cocktails and more.

As with lemon verbena, you can line a cake tin with the leaves, pour in the batter and cook: once cooled, peel off and discard the leaves. The result will be beautifully fragrant.

Leaves can keep in the fridge for a week and freeze really well.

SHISO

Perilla frutescens

Hardy annual

✄ Late spring until early autumn

75cm (30in)

Affinities

Seafood, especially prawns (shrimp)

Eggs

Rice

Noodles

Aubergines (eggplant)

Avocado

Courgettes (zucchini)

Cucumber

Radishes

Tomatoes

Apples

Pears

Stone fruit

Lemongrass

Parsley

Shiso, aka perilla, forms a rope bridge of flavour that spans the gap between mint and cumin. As the weather warms, the leaves slide along the spectrum towards cumin, picking up a little cinnamon along the way; when it's cooler, it has more parsley and mint in its warm flavour. Tall, elegant, and beautiful enough to be grown as a foliage plant for flower arrangements, shiso's tooth-edged, slightly crinkly leaves catch the eye through the late spring and summer. Part of the mint family, it possesses a flavour of generous proportions, and carries it even in the flowers borne from mid summer. Native to much of Asia, shiso is widely used in Chinese and Japanese cooking in particular: you may be familiar with it in sushi.

Varieties
Lime green and deep purple variations.

How to grow
Sow shiso direct from mid spring, into warm, well-drained soil: it can take time to germinate, but once underway it grows quickly in a sunny spot, with a little water through the driest of spells.

The flowers are beautiful and delicious, but their production slows down that of the leaves, and reduces their intensity and flavour; either do as I do, and grow great swathes so that you can leave some to flower and some to pick, or pinch out the tops to keep the plants busy and productive. If the winter is mild and you allow some plants to go to seed, expect free plants the following year.

Harvesting
You can be fairly industrial in harvesting shiso by cutting it low and storing it in a vase to use later, but if you snip just above a leaf joint it will recover more quickly. If pinching out any buds or flowers, use them too as they carry much of the flavour of the leaves.

When/how to use
Shiso is delicate, so add it late to anything cooked or use it raw. The texture can be a little dry and papery; shred it finely to get the flavour and soften the texture. Use sparingly in leafy salads, generously with aubergines, grilled or barbecued prawns, and with eggs and avocado.

It is related to mint and basil, and you can be confident in using where either finds a happy home: try it first with tomatoes, and then in a shiso mojito. Actually, reverse that.

Shiso also combines well with peaches and nectarines, pear and apple. I use it a fair bit in pickles and vinegars; be aware that it can turn vinegar, wine and citrus juice purple.

It is one you really have to try tempura-ed.

SORREL

Rumex acetosa

Hardy perennial

✂ Summer to early winter

60cm (24in) tall

Affinities

Chicken

Lamb

Fish

Seafood

Butter

Cream

Eggs

Lentils

Carrots

Cucumber

Leeks

Peas

Potatoes

Spinach

Tomatoes

Sorrel hits me – with a wincing eye and a sharp jolt – right in that sour spot that gooseberries and rhubarb like to make their home. You could argue it's more of a salad leaf or even a leafy vegetable than a herb, and that its uses are relatively few, and yet it somehow grasped my biased hand and made it into this book's castle as the drawbridge came up, purely on the grounds that I love it. Pecking a fork into a pan of sorrel that's giving up the ghost to the heat of just-cooked nutty new potatoes, butter and salt is one of the great 'summer's here' pleasures.

Varieties

Buckler-leaved and Broad-leaved sorrel are the best for flavour and texture.

How to grow

Sorrel is a perennial grown mostly as an annual for the most succulent leaves. Sow direct in spring: as they grow, you can always thin (end eat) the plants if you want wider spacing. Semi-shade is ideal. Water through dry periods to avoid them going to seed; although the seeds of Buckler-leaved sorrel are little pale yellow discs of the most intense lemon, so do let a few go.

Harvesting

Snip off leaves as you need them, and/or cut the plant back to 6cm (2½in) to encourage fresh growth.

When/how to use

Tender to the point of vulnerability, sorrel, like spinach, goes from skipful to thimbleful in any kind of heat and makes a happy partner for oily fish and lamb, potatoes and eggs in a completely distinctive way; when young and small, the leaves bring sharp punctuation to leafy salads. Strip out the central vein of larger leaves and chop before using. The bold green of the leaves will turn the khaki of the last Mod in town's parka, but the flavour remains.

Sorrel makes a wonderful soup, and it creams beautifully with or without spinach (or indeed parsley) to go with poached eggs on toast. There is a special seasonal pleasure in tossing handfuls of chopped sorrel into just-cooked new potatoes, with a lot of butter, and allowing it to wilt into its own sauce. Although harvestable into autumn, be aware that the leaves can become a little less succulent and less brightly flavoured as the season rolls on.

SWEET CICELY

Myrrhis odorata

Hardy perennial

✂ Early spring to autumn

1m (3ft) tall

Affinities

Chicken

Seafood, especially scallops

Asparagus

Carrots

Chard

Courgettes (zucchini)

Parsnips

Apricots

Gooseberries

Peaches and nectarines

Rhubarb

Mint

Lemon verbena

Sweet cicely has so much to recommend it. A perennial, it comes out lively and bright at the first sign of spring, it's happy in dampish ground, in half-shade, and it requires nothing from you other than an admiring gaze. All parts of it are edible: the leaves, roots, flowers and seeds carry a delicious, sweet gentle aniseed flavour.

It looks like a fern whose leaves have fanned out having reached some imaginary ceiling. It is of the parsley family, and grows to anywhere from 50–120cm (20–50in) tall, producing until well into autumn. It flowers early in spring, drawing pollinators into the garden, before the flowers turn to long, slim and very beautiful seeds. Pinch these seeds off while they are green for the kitchen, or allow them to fall where new plants will spring forth the following year.

Varieties
Generic.

How to grow
Sweet cicely can be a pain to get started: the seeds require a good spell of cold to germinate, so either allow seeds to fall naturally from the plant and produce new plants from there, freeze the seeds for a couple of months before sowing, or short-cut all that and start with a plant. Grow in semi-shade. Cut back the flower stems after they produce seeds if you want to encourage a new flush of leaves.

Harvesting
Pick leaves and seeds as you need them.

When/how to use
More than anything, I love to infuse the leaves and seeds in sugar syrup or vodka: the flavour leaches out so well. The leaves are superb thinly sliced and not heavily present in a leafy salad, and even quickly stir-fried, especially with asparagus which happily springs forth just in time to accompany.

Sweet cicely was commonly used with sharp fruits such as rhubarb and gooseberries; it lends a sweet aniseed that reads on the tongue as sweetness without the anise, and allows you to use less sugar than you ordinarily might.

Sweet cicely goes limp quickly; you might get it to last five days in the fridge.

TARRAGON

Artemisia dracunculus

Tender perennial

✂ Late spring to autumn

90cm (35in) tall

Affinities

Chicken

Fish, especially meaty halibut

Scallops

Dairy

Eggs

Asparagus

Courgettes (zucchini)

Globe artichokes

Green beans

Potatoes

Tomatoes

Citrus

Most other soft herbs

Gin

Vinegar

When I say tarragon, I mean French tarragon, the untidy, spindly perennial, rarely looking quite like it has the wherewithal to survive a strong gust. Its flavour is quite peculiar: on the face of it, it is driven by aniseed, backed up by a little of what mint has, a vague milky pepperiness too, but it has a fine citrusy brightness alongside something that is similar to – but not quite – smoky.

It is classically paired with chicken, though I use it as much with tomatoes, green beans and in potato salads. It is one of the best soft-leaved herbs for making a syrup, and in turn the excellent cocktail on page 264. And tarragon vinegar is something you should never be without.

Varieties
Grow only French tarragon. The Russian variety may be more vigorous, but who wants a pale tribute band rather than the real thing. Mexican tarragon (*Tagetes lucida*) is a different thing altogether, and marvellous (page 86).

How to grow
Start with a plant, or from cuttings. Sun and a rich, well-drained soil are essentials. Feed it regularly with compost and/or liquid feed though the summer. Tarragon likes a spell of winter chill, so if you are growing it in containers don't be tempted to tuck the pot somewhere warm over winter. It's worth lifting tarragon every few years and dividing it into two or three to reinvigorate it.

Harvesting
Harvest as and when you like, leaving at least half to allow it to regrow. The intensity of its flavour varies with the seasons; spring leaves are sweeter, and the hotter the sun, the more intense the flavour.

When/how to use
Tarragon tends to lose its flavour if cooked for too long, although cast into a roasting chicken's cavity, slipped under the skin with butter, or in a shallow bath of cider beneath it seem to be exceptions. French tarragon combines beautifully with other herbs, acting – as chervil and sweet cicely can – as a catalyser, magnifying the qualities of those it is with. Parsley, lemon thyme and chives are my three favourites, in any combination, with it.

Use immediately; tarragon keeps for a few days only in the fridge but the flavour loses intensity.

THYME

Thymus vulgaris
Hardy perennial
✂ Year round
60cm (24in) tall

Affinities

Almost anything, but
especially:
Bacon
Beef
Chicken
Lamb
Rabbit
Fish
Shellfish
Goat's cheese
Eggs
Aubergines (eggplant)
Cabbage
Garlic
Leeks
Olives
Onions
Sweetcorn
Tomatoes
Apples
Lemons
Oranges
Pears
Rhubarb
Chocolate
Mushrooms

Thyme is easy to love too hard. Its green, woody savouriness goes so very well with so very much that the temptation is to keep harvesting, your plants becoming stubby monuments to your love. For this reason alone, I buy a fair amount of the thyme I use and grow my favourite varieties to use when that extra few degrees of excellence will make a difference. I suggest you do the same. Lemon and orange thymes are utterly indispensable, leaning that familiar thyminess towards spring or autumn, cheery or calm.

Varieties
A good broad-leaved common thyme (Tabor is a favourite), lemon and orange thymes are essential. Spring Bright is special.

How to grow
Thyme is very easy to grow, as long as it has sun, a well-drained soil and you don't hammer it too hard with the scissors. Prune back by a third in spring once leaves have re-emerged, and after flowering, to prevent legginess and encourage fresh bushy growth. Liquid feed container plants fortnightly in summer.

Harvesting
Cut anywhere up to halfway down the stems, taking no more than a third of what's on offer at a time. Or snip off a couple of centimetres of fresh new growth, keeping the plant tight and tidy, and encourage it to grow more. While growth can be vigorous in the sunny months, it slows dramatically in winter, so pick less then.

When/how to use
I rarely make a savoury tart without thyme. It brings out the best in onions, joining the dots with vegetables in the tart's custard, bringing an earthy, savoury depth of flavour. Its piney, lightly smoky, thinly camphorous flavour seems to enhance anything, whether meat, fish, vegetable or fruit. I use orange and lemon thymes almost as much as familiar thyme: the former is one of my favourites with rhubarb, infused in milk, in cakes or ice cream, while the latter is incredible on roasting apricots, chicken or infused in sugar syrup for cocktails. Occasionally, I use it when making stock, but only if I'm also using bay, otherwise it can drive a peculiar bus through the whole.

Thyme works beautifully in soups, stews and braises: it brings a special magic solo or in tandem with others, especially rosemary, marjoram and bay. Add it at any stage: early for a wider flavour, or late for an altogether brighter impression.

Thyme is excellent added when making fresh pasta – the flavour endures and the texture isn't so woody as to annoy.

It's a good idea to strip the leaves from unpalatable woodier stems, discarding the stems, or if the stems are soft enough, finely chop them and use alongside the leaves. If you would rather remove the stems from a stew or similar once cooked, tie them into a bunch for easy retrieval.

If fresh, thyme stores for two weeks in the fridge.

OTHER FAVOURITES

The following herbs didn't make it onto the main list in the Herbs to Grow and Eat section as their use is fairly limited, and/or they can't be grown well in temperate climates; however, I wouldn't be without them.

Angelica

I rarely use angelica, though I love it when I do and I won't do without it in the garden. Its flavour is peculiarly reminiscent of gin, most particularly its juniper element. The stems and leaves are edible, though for the most part unappetizing: where the stems shine are in combination with rhubarb and other sharp fruit, where its effect is to sweeten and somehow accentuate the flavour of the fruit. The stems are very good candied too. Easy to grow, either from seed or start with a plant, as long as you give it a fairly shady spot and water well while establishing and through dry spells. Collect seed after it has flowered (usually in year two, but sometimes later) or allow it to self-seed as it is a biennial; once it has set seed it dies.

Avocado leaves

Widely used throughout central and southern Mexico, avocado leaves are one of those herbs better dried than fresh. The drying/toasting process accentuates their gentle anise flavour, and leaves them ready to be infused in soups, stews and sauces or ground to a dust for livening guacamole or fish. If you can find the leaves fresh, they are good for wrapping fish, or refried beans before cooking is a good variation. Lightly toast the leaves before use.

Bergamot

This is not the Earl Grey scented citrus, the bergamot orange, but the beautiful perennial herb *Monarda didyma*, with punchy leaves that carry just about the best approximation there is for mixed herbs in one place. It is a superb coming together of – in ascending order of impact – rosemary, both savories, oregano, thyme and marjoram, with citrus. The plant is beautiful, throwing up extraordinary bold flowers in mid summer, that add a serious splash of claret to the garden. Try lemon bergamot – an annual – for its very lemony leaves.

Blackcurrant leaves

I seem to spend half my life with the pad of my thumb making soft circles against the tip of my first two fingers, a leaf between them. And in early spring, that leaf is likely to be blackcurrant. They carry a rosier version of the fruit's flavour, that infuses beautifully. As long as you go easy and take a couple of handfuls of leaves from across the whole plant, it won't affect the plant negatively, nor the fruit harvest. The flavour is at its best before summer hits. (Pictured opposite.)

Curry leaf

This beautifully aromatic herb is almost a spice by virtue of it being most widely available in the UK as a dried leaf, rather than fresh, but either way, I have let it through the gates of this book as I use it so much and I guess mostly as a halfway house that's very slightly more herb than spice. The leaves' flavour is pungent, nutty, unsurprisingly curryish but with a slight lemon backbeat, and is used widely across southern India especially. I usually warm the leaves in a dry pan to stir up those aromatics. The leaves make an excellent vinegar too. You can grow this tropical citrus plant in European latitudes but it has to be indoors and they do take a little mollycoddling.

English mace

A relatively unknown perennial herb with thin, stiff branches topped by small daisy-like flowers in summer. The leaves carry a superb soft yet lively scent and flavour – imagine thyme, caraway and mint had a child. Although mild, English mace is peculiarly present so use it sparingly. I use it most often in soups, eggs and find it particularly good with chicken.

Epazote

If ever a herb split a room faster than someone singing 'Summertime' at an after-pub party, it's epazote. Native of south and central Mexico, I think of epazote as two distinct herbs: fresh and dried. If I told you its scent and taste is a curious blend of savory, mint, a hint of citrus and putty, you might be semi-curious at best; let me further tell you that fresh the leaves are worse than abysmal, but dried the leaves are quite something – somehow bitter and pungent, yet refreshing. It is oddly addictive. Go lightly with it and add it late with only 15 minutes' cooking, in stews and soups, in salsas and in spicy bean dishes. It is surprisingly good with fish too.

Fig leaves

Fig leaves are an ingredient it's easy to overlook. Like banana leaves, they seem to get the job of wrapping fish or infusing rice, and while they do it beautifully, it's not something that hits my kitchen priority list. In recent years, I have come to love using these leaves – they're like Pat Jennings' gloves – to infuse as I might bay, most often in milk and cream.

Unless you are using them to wrap food, and that fresh flexibility is key, the first step to getting the best from them is to toast them. I use a slow oven where the intensity of heat is even (page 119).

Young leaves are best, but even those in their midlife will do perfectly well.

Hyssop

Yet another of my favourite herbs that I use only occasionally. It looks like a slightly more refined relative of rosemary, with a flavour that while resinous is also citrusy-sour, with bitter hints and a touch of mint. It is perhaps at its best with fatty, rich, creamy or salty foods. I use it most in long-cooked stews and similar, in burgers and sometimes when making za'atar, as it is thought by many to be the authentic, traditional herb for it.

Makrut (kaffir) lime leaves

It's high time we adopted more widely the term makrut lime or Thai lime in place of the commonly used kaffir lime. I know no one uses it with intention, but there are terms we ought to leave to history. I use the familiar term here only for clarity, to help us step across the threshold from one to the other with common understanding as to what leaves, fruit and plant we are referring. The sweet aromatic citrusy flavour and scent of the leaves is perhaps best known to most in Thai green curries. It is by no means heavy-handed but very present nonetheless. As with bay and blackcurrant leaves, the leaves are usually infused to release their flavour, though if you cut out the central rib, roll up the two halves and chiffonade very finely, it has the effect of softening the leathery texture, making it perfect to scatter on noodle dishes and so on.

Mexican oregano

I'm fairly sure there's not a better dried herb than Mexican oregano: it adds depth when added early, but still retains brightness in the final tasting. It shares some flavour characteristics with familiar oregano, hence its common name, but is a different species (*Lippia graveolens*). It is considerably more citrusy, grassy and even occasionally has a distant hint of liquorice. It is particularly good with lamb and tomatoes, and is most widely available in dried form, though it is easy to grow and very good. I use it most often with garlic and salt in a lively rub for meat or fish, or in a dressing.

Mexican tarragon

You are unlikely to find Mexican tarragon (*Tagetes lucida*) to buy in the shops so try to persuade yourself to grow some: its flavour is sweeter, more intensely aniseed and is generally a little coarser than French tarragon, but that's no bad thing. Its flowers are also very good to eat. It is a heat-loving marigold, so if you grow it keep it under cover or in the house unless you have mild winters. Use as you would French tarragon: it makes an especially fine vinegar.

Pineapple sage

The leaves of pineapple sage have one of my favourite scents in the garden. Bright, pineappley, yet rich and deep in that way sage – its relative – makes its own. It makes a superb herb syrup and herb sugar, and even if there are not a multitude of other uses to which it leans, in these forms it can do so much good in cakes, cocktails, biscuits, crumbles, and other desserts. And it's a beauty in the garden. It's a perennial, so a plant should last you for years.

Vietnamese coriander

Aka laksa leaf, this is a wonderful, fragrant plant with all the punch of coriander with plenty of bright lemon/lime and a little mint thrown in. It has so much going for it, and despite growing it for many many years, I confess I have plenty to explore with it still. I use it most in laksa, noodle dishes, and shredded and scattered over tomato and chickpea salads; the leaves don't take well to heat, so I add them on serving. Easy to grow and prolific. (Pictured on page 84.)

Wild garlic

Every spring, the damp, half-shade of the beech woods near where I live feel the footsteps of those who know the magic that lies within. You'll see people with baskets, a sharp knife and a searching gaze looking for clusters of wild garlic, the first sign that winter really will soon be behind us. Its wide green tongues may resemble other plants but the scent of the leaves – and the woods when the humidity is just so – is unmistakable. Grow it yourself in similar conditions if you like, but it's so much nicer stepping out into the semi-wild and picking a little of what nature offers in abundance. (Pictured opposite.)

If you were expecting to see lemon balm: No.

INFUSIONS, BLENDS
AND SAUCES

SHISO PICKLED CUCUMBER

Shiso's flavour – all soft cumin and mild mint – pairs beautifully with cucumber, in salads, shrubs and here in this quick pickle. Its crêpe paper texture is best softened by fine slicing – a good chiffonade – which also helps release its flavour quickly into the vinegar for the cucumber to pick up. And if you use the deep purple variety, expect slow clouds of pink to transform the colour of the vinegar.

Fills 1 x 700ml (1¼ pints) jar

480ml (16fl oz) white wine vinegar

85g (3oz) caster (superfine) sugar

2 tbsp sea salt

12 black peppercorns

a few thin slices of ginger

1 garlic clove, thinly sliced

1 thin red chilli, sliced lengthways and deseeded

1 good-sized cucumber, peeled and cut into 3mm (⅛in) half moons

8 large leaves of shiso, rolled and thinly sliced

Have a sterilized jar ready.

In a pan, bring the vinegar, sugar, salt, peppercorns and ginger to a simmer, stirring to dissolve; simmer for 10 minutes.

Put the garlic, chilli, half the cucumber and half the shiso into the jar. Pour two-thirds of the vinegar in, add the rest of the cucumber and shiso and top with the remaining vinegar. Refrigerate once cool.

This should be excellent after a day, once the shiso loses a little pigment and flavour to the vinegar, and lasts for a week or so, after which the cucumber's texture becomes a little gummy.

INDIAN GREEN CHUTNEY

A friend told me that the surest sign of middle age is when you stand in front of the mirror wearing your favourite shorts and Baden-Powell is staring back. The consolation of that moment occurring to me is that at least it indicated a summer deserving of shorts; a summer where chillies ripened full and plentiful. Your choice of chilli here is crucial: a lively, slim Thai chilli is ideal – something with heat but not too much volume. Start with one; you can always add more at the end if it lacks punch. And punch it must have: with its fresh liveliness and chilli slap, this should wake everything – including the eater – fully up. As a side to main dishes, to have with flatbreads, naan breads or poppadoms, this quick-to-make chutney is hard to beat. Add mint if you fancy, in about 3:1 coriander to mint ratio. The pinch of ground green cardamon is a lovely variation, as is a little fresh coconut.

Makes a small jarful

2 garlic cloves, finely chopped

1 tbsp grated fresh ginger

1 tbsp caster (superfine) sugar

1–3 fresh green chillies, deseeded if you want less heat

big bunch of coriander (cilantro), roughly chopped

juice of 1 lemon

good pinch of ground cumin

pinch of ground green cardamon (optional)

good pinch of salt

Have a sterilized jar ready.

Place all the ingredients in a blender and pulse until smooth. Taste and adjust the seasoning if needed.

Keeps in the fridge for a couple of days.

NECTARINE AND LIME LEAF CHUTNEY

What is the collective term for supermarket nectarines…? An impersonation? An apology? A scandal of nectarines; yes, that'll do. Even a week after buying it, a 'ripen at home' nectarine can still likely withstand a day of Ashes cricket. Cooking is their only salvation, and this combination with lime leaves is really special. There isn't a cheese or cold meat that this won't go beautifully with.

Makes a large jarful

1kg (2lb 4oz) nectarines (about 10 fruit), stoned and diced

1 red onion, diced

250ml (9fl oz) apple cider vinegar

180g (6oz) caster (superfine) sugar

1 tsp salt

½ tsp ground turmeric

1 tsp cumin seeds

2 tbsp black mustard seeds

1 tsp ground ginger

3–5 makrut lime leaves, depending on size, very thinly sliced

2 tbsp cornflour (cornstarch)

Get your jar(s) ready – sterilized and dry.

Place the nectarines and onion in a large, heavy-based, stainless steel pan, along with the vinegar and sugar. Bring to simmering point, stirring occasionally, then add the salt, spices and lime leaves and simmer for 15–30 minutes until the fruit has softened but still has a little firmness.

Meanwhile, mix the cornflour (cornstarch) with just enough water to turn it into Tippex. Add to the chutney and cook for a further 5 minutes, stirring often, until the chutney thickens.

Spoon into your jar(s) and seal. Allow the flavours to develop for a fortnight or so before using. Once open, store in the fridge where it should keep for a few months.

PISTOU

The only thing that sets pistou apart from pesto is a handful of pine nuts, yet it feels like something very different. Where pesto has everything it needs to be itself, pistou is incomplete, becoming itself in the company of another, transforming the other in the process. This is perfectly demonstrated in the way it transports minestrone into pistou soup (page 133). Added late, it seasons and elevates, bringing basil's flavour without it being lost in cooking.

Use this to finish soups, casseroles and stews, just on serving. If appearances matter, blanch the basil in boiling water for 5 seconds and plunge it into iced water to retain its bright colour. By all means make this with a pestle and mortar if you prefer.

Makes a small jarful

50g (2oz) basil leaves and stalks

1 large garlic clove, finely chopped

75ml (3fl oz) extra virgin olive oil

20g (¾oz) Parmesan, finely grated

sea salt and freshly ground black pepper

Have a sterilized jar ready.

Place all the ingredients in a blender and pulse until smooth. Taste and season to taste. Stores in the fridge for a fortnight or so.

CHERMOULA

This is a cracker of a sauce common in the countries of coastal North Africa.
I have a weakness for chermoula with prawns (page 200) and other seafood,
but it is not hard to make a friend of; chicken and aubergines are particularly
happy in its company.

As with all these sauces and blends, you should feel free to experiment:
I added a little grated ginger and the zest of the juiced lemon half, having seen
it in a Diana Henry recipe, and it's a superb variation.

Makes a small jarful

small bunch of coriander
(cilantro), roughly chopped

small bunch of parsley,
roughly chopped

2 garlic cloves, peeled

1 small red chilli,
destemmed

50ml (2fl oz) olive oil

juice of ½ lemon

2 tsp smoked paprika

1 tsp ground cumin

sea salt and freshly ground
black pepper

Finely chop the herbs, garlic and chilli together (or use a blender if it has a small
capacity), then whisk in the oil, lemon juice, spices and seasoning. Keep in the
fridge for a day or two.

DILL MUSTARD SAUCE

Gravadlax (page 190) is often served with a sauce like this – full of punch
and plenty of dill – and while it does go beautifully with cured fish, it's equally
special on boiled new potatoes, or with ham and eggs.

Makes a small jarful

3 tbsp Dijon mustard

1 tbsp runny honey

juice of ½ lemon

generous pinch of salt

3 tbsp olive oil

20g (¾oz) dill, thick stalks
removed, roughly chopped

Mix together the mustard, honey, lemon juice and salt.

Whisk in the oil and stir in the dill. Keeps in the fridge for a day or two.

ADJIKA

This incredible sauce/dip from Georgia is intense, poky, bright and full-on. Heat, salt, garlic and oil are the constants that you can ad-lib around, though I rarely make this without mint. Lemon verbena brings perfume and a cool breeze; coriander is altogether calmer. Once you feel confident with this, do play as you like: it's perfectly usual for me to make this drier or even on the edge of becoming an oil. It's up to you what proportions of mint to lemon verbena make up the 90g (3 ¼ oz) – I usually go for 55g/35g (2/1 ¼ oz). As with many comings-together of salt, heat and herb, you'll find that ideas for using it Catherine-wheel from your mind as you taste it.

Makes a small jarful

90g (3 ¼ oz) mint and lemon verbena

3 large green, mid-heat chillies

4 large garlic cloves, peeled

30g (1oz) salt

20ml (¾ fl oz) olive oil

20ml (¾ fl oz) walnut oil

Have a sterilized jar ready.

Strip the leaves from the mint and lemon verbena stems and discard the stems. Place all the ingredients in a blender and blitz on high speed.

Store in the fridge, where it should keep for at least a couple of weeks.

PESTO

They say there is no sex better than the sex your ex is enjoying with their new partner in your tormented imagination; similarly, there is no palaver greater than the imagined palaver involved in making pesto. The reality (at least in pesto's case) couldn't be more different, and the pay-off is so infinitely disproportionate to the effort involved. That said, hunger-induced laziness gets the better of me now and again and I use the food processor, when pesto is one of those few instances when a mortar and pestle makes such a difference to the result.

Makes a small jarful

big bunch of basil, leaves picked (you want about 120g/4oz leaves)

1 garlic clove, finely chopped

30g (1oz) pine nuts, toasted in a dry frying pan over a medium heat until golden

150ml (5fl oz) very good olive oil, plus more to seal

50g (2oz) pecorino or Parmesan, freshly grated (a mix of both is nice)

sea salt and freshly ground black pepper

Put the basil and garlic into a food processor (or use a pestle and mortar) with a big pinch of salt and pulse or pound to a rough green paste. Add the pine nuts and pulse or pound, retaining some texture to the nuts.

Add the oil gradually, and pulse or stir until it's all incorporated. Stir in the cheese and check the seasoning, adding salt and pepper to taste. Transfer to a jar.

If not using straight away, place the pesto in a sterilized jar and cover with a little olive oil, making sure it is completely submerged. It will keep well in the fridge for about a week.

GREEN SAUCE

Of the many sauces that go under this name, this might be the quickest and easiest to create. It is a real punchy, refreshing go-to, enlivening pretty much anything at a barbecue, be it fish, fowl, red meat or vegetable. It also wakes pork tacos up a treat (page 217).

Makes a small jarful

6 large garlic cloves, peeled

50g (2oz) coriander (cilantro)

juice of 4 limes and the finely grated zest of 2

Place everything in a blender and whizz until semi-smooth.

Keeps in the fridge for a day or two.

GREEN SEASONING

This Caribbean sauce is all about freshness and heat, and while you'll find as many variations on this as there are people on those islands, the inarguable is that it be full of lime, bright onion and to not hold back on the chilli. Thyme and coriander (and their Caribbean variations) are the usual herbs, but embellish as you wish: I imagine Vietnamese coriander and lime leaves would make a very different but similarly pleasing combination. Unusually, considering it has so much coriander leaf and spring onions, green seasoning is commonly used as a marinade, added early in the cooking process. Try the lamb rundown on page 213 and you'll see just how well it works.

Makes a small jarful

3 garlic cloves, finely chopped

juice of ½ lime

1 bunch of spring onions (scallions), thinly sliced

small bunch of coriander (cilantro), roughly chopped

small bunch of fresh thyme, leaves picked

1 fresh green chilli (or use a Scotch Bonnet for extra flavour and lots of extra heat)

1 tsp salt

Place all the ingredients in a blender and whizz to make a not-quite-smooth sauce.

Keeps in the fridge for a day or two.

SALSA VERDE

With its oily acidity, salsa verde has so much of the vinaigrette about it, yet is barely a sauce in reality, with the merest oiliness keeping it mobile.

Parsley is the beating heart of a good salsa verde, around which to adapt to what you have and what it is accompanying – perhaps upping the mint for lamb, the fennel fronds for fish, basil for roasted vegetables etc. I often add a finely diced shallot; sometimes a few chopped cornichons.

If you wish to start an argument, tell someone how you make salsa verde. It is, you will be told, the wrong way. Some swear by a mortar and pestle, others the food processor. At the risk of causing a pile-on, I prefer the chop chop chop of below as it gives a soft coarseness with pops of each flavour, but these quantities work beautifully – if differently – whichever method you prefer.

Makes a medium jarful

big bunch of flat-leaf parsley, leaves only

small bunch of basil or mint, leaves only (or use a combination)

4 anchovies, rinsed if packed in salt and finely chopped

2 tbsp salted capers, rinsed and roughly chopped

2 garlic cloves, finely chopped

1 tbsp Dijon mustard

2 tbsp red wine vinegar or lemon juice

About 100ml (3½fl oz) good-quality extra virgin olive oil, plus more to seal

sea salt and freshly ground black pepper

Chop the herbs, anchovies, capers and garlic with a large knife all together on a big board, then tip into a bowl.

Stir in the mustard and vinegar, then mix in about 100ml (3½fl oz) of the oil until you achieve your desired consistency. Taste and add more vinegar/lemon if you like, plus salt and pepper to taste.

Store in a jar with a thin layer of oil on the top in the fridge. Keeps for a day or two.

GOOSEBERRY SALSA

A friend who lived on Exmoor for a couple of decades noted that people in the delightfully isolated villages in his area were often known for a single quality. It might be 'the guy who can fix a traction engine', 'she used to keep ocelots' or 'he's got the best set of socket spanners for miles around'. My friend made (awful) home brew once in his life, during his first winter in the village, and was known for the decades that followed as The Home Brew Man. Thanks to my friend Emma T, who champions this to anyone who crosses her path, there are countless households to whom I am The Gooseberry Salsa Man. I've been making this recipe – firstly, with mint, chives and a couple of leaves of lovage – for a good few years, and this is the latest incarnation. Mint, makrut lime and sweet cicely make this as bright as frost in May, and if you haven't got sweet cicely, use another sweetly aniseedy herb such as fennel.

Try this with mackerel (smoked or otherwise), goose, duck or pork.

Serves 4

4 tbsp caster (superfine) sugar

3 tbsp white wine vinegar

150g (5oz) gooseberries, topped and tailed

3 shallots, thinly sliced

grated zest and juice of 1 small lime

small handful of mint, finely shredded

small handful of sweet cicely, finely chopped

2 makrut lime leaves, very finely shredded

sea salt and freshly ground black pepper

Put the sugar, a good pinch of salt and a few twists of pepper and the vinegar into a pan and bring slowly to a simmer.

Add the gooseberries and gently cook, stirring frequently, for a couple of minutes only – you want the process of cooking just to begin rather than to soften the fruit. Take off the heat and allow to cool.

Stir in the shallots, lime zest and juice and the herbs and refrigerate for a couple of hours or more before serving.

CHIMICHURRI

From the ingredients, you could be forgiven for thinking chimichurri is just a salsa verde with a parting on the other side: the base of red wine vinegar, olive oil, parsley and garlic is shared, but the ratios, the shift in heat from mustard to chilli and the earthiness of the oregano rather than the basil or mint make this Basque/Argentinian sauce so very different.

Chimichurri is perfect with all things meat, especially if smoke and wood are involved, but I love it equally with roasted vegetables, with fish and crisp, hot potatoes, such as the deep-fried rosemary potatoes on page 137.

Tximitxurri means a mix of everything, so experiment: thyme, marjoram and even savory are superb in place of the oregano, coriander alongside the parsley, spring onions rather than the shallot, and the degree of chilli heat is very much your preference and might come from a fresh chilli.

At the risk of being thrown in the village stocks for heresy, there's nothing wrong with blending the ingredients into a bright green smooth sauce if you prefer. It will be different, and I prefer it as is, but sometimes life requires a short cut.

Makes a medium jarful

4 tbsp red wine vinegar

½ tsp salt

2 garlic cloves, finely chopped

1 small shallot, finely chopped (or use ½ bunch of trimmed spring onions/scallions)

½ tsp chilli flakes, or more to taste

1 tsp good-quality dried oregano

small bunch of parsley, finely chopped

2 tbsp fresh oregano (optional)

6 tbsp extra virgin olive oil

sea salt and freshly ground black pepper

Mix together the vinegar, salt, garlic and shallot and put to one side for 10 minutes.

Stir in the rest of the ingredients and allow the flavours to get to know each other for an hour or so before serving. Keeps in the fridge for a day or two.

VIETNAMESE CORIANDER, MAKRUT LIME AND CURRY LEAF SALT

I spent all of 75 hours being pleased as punch at coming up with this superb herb salt combination, before seeing an idea for the very same combination in my excellent friend Catherine Phipps' book *Leaf*. I must've subliminally taken it in; her 'She's So Fine', to my 'My Sweet Lord'. Catherine has kindly allowed me to semi-steal it here, taking her combination idea and putting quantities to it that I hope she (and you) will enjoy.

This is a wonderfully bright and breezy salt – the lemon of the Vietnamese coriander and the lime of the makrut leaves sitting beautifully with the salt, all held in line by the earthiness of the curry leaves. By all means, do without the curry leaves if you fancy the lights on full beam. Accuracy in leaf numbers isn't crucial (no one's going to count dried curry leaves) but the mathematic symmetry helps me remember without reaching for the recipe.

As with so many sugars and salts, you start by using them very specifically – as part of a crust on baked cod, finishing a laksa, on sweet potato chips – and then find almost anything gets a dusting once you have a taste for it.

Makes a small jarful

2 makrut lime leaves

22 Vietnamese coriander leaves

44 dried curry leaves

40g (1 ½ oz) coarse sea salt

Toast the lime leaves in a hot pan until they dry a little, then add the coriander leaves; when they become papery and limp remove them all, and toast the curry leaves until their scent makes your stomach rumble.

Place the leaves and salt (add last to weigh down the herbs) in a coffee/spice grinder and whizz thoroughly; the change in tone to single-note zing will tell you when it's ready. If there are any remnants left unreduced, stir and whizz briefly again.

You can dry this, as in the marjoram and chive salt recipe on page 104, but the brightness here deserves to be used quickly, so I tend to use it wet, hence the lesser amount I make.

MARJORAM AND CHIVE FLOWER SALT

Once in a while, an ingredient tugs at your collar. You'll be watching the match, chatting to a loved one, engrossed at the cinema, and a biplane will fly across your mind trailing a ribbon that says, 'I wonder what that would be like on hot chips' or 'if I sprinkled that on a steak before frying as well as after…' This salt is one of those.

It started colonizing my mind when I was drying a batch. The unmistakeable scent – pickled onion Monster Munch, the forge in which my unfortunate frame was cast – crept from oven to nose, and I was sold.

How you dry this salt is everything. Leave it for a few days on greaseproof paper to slow-dry on a sunny window sill and its flavour is delightfully seaweedy; dry in a very low oven for 15 minutes (more if needed) and it'll be a little brighter. Try half a batch of both and see which you prefer.

Makes a small jarful

17g (⅔oz) marjoram leaves

12 chive flower heads

60g (2¼oz) coarse sea salt

Place the leaves, 8 of the chive flowers and the salt (add last to weigh down the herbs) in a coffee/spice grinder and whizz thoroughly: the change in tone from clatter to dentist drill tells you when it's as it should be. If there are any remnants left unreduced, stir and whizz briefly again.

For the oven-dry method, spread out (the salt, not you) on baking parchment on a baking sheet, and place in a very low oven; 110°C (230°F) or so is good. After 10–15 minutes it should lighten in colour. Scratch it up a little with a fork to expose the parts that are still a little damp and return to the oven. After 15–20 minutes it should be fairly dry. Allow to cool, add the remaining chive flowers (broken up a little), then jar immediately and try to focus on whatever else the day brings.

BASIL SUGAR

Unless you've grown it yourself or it's organic, I'd wash a herb like basil. It's impossible to get completely dry, which in combination with the fleshiness of its leaves makes it well suited to making a herb sugar purée rather than a dust. This intense dark sugar is wonderful dotted on goat's cheese, stone fruit and flavouring a tall glass of fizz.

Makes a small jarful

50g (2oz) basil

50g (2oz) caster (superfine) sugar

Wash the basil and shake free of most of the water. Lay out on a double layer of kitchen paper, dab with another double layer until it's as dry as you can make it. Place in a coffee/spice grinder and add the sugar. Whizz, stopping now and again to stir some of the purée on to the top to encourage the unincorporated leaves to fall under the blades.

Once a fairly consistent purée forms, scrape out into a jar. It should keep for a week or two in the fridge.

KOREAN MINT SUGAR

My journey to big school was usually punctuated by a visit to the sweet shop. Spacedust and other sherbetty treats were eternal favourites, and while this misses the sourness of most of those, it has that same lick-the-end-of-your-finger-and-dip-it-in-ness in spades. Going heavier on the herb makes for a more intense flavour, though a wetter sugar; good if you are going to use it within a day or two. Sprinkle this on peaches and other stone fruit, dust it on cocktails, or on yoghurt… (Pictured opposite.)

Makes a small jarful

40g (1½oz) Korean mint leaves

50g (2oz) caster (superfine) sugar

Whizz the leaves and sugar in a coffee/spice blender until a smoothish paste forms. Smear this thinnishly over a piece of baking parchment and place on a baking sheet in a low oven; 110°C (230°F) or so is good. After 10–15 minutes it should lighten in colour. Scratch it up a little with a fork to expose the parts that are still a little damp and return to the oven. After 15–20 minutes it should be fairly dry. Remove from the oven, allow to cool and whizz again in the blender to create a fine dust.

PICADA

Hello Catalonia. Although picada shares a thread with pesto, it is not really a sauce at all; rather, a loose friendship that transforms when added late to a braise, stew or when making cooking juices into a sauce, thickening as it enlivens.

Ask four people and you will get five opinions of what absolutely has to be in picada, and chances are they are all fine ideas. I rarely make it the same twice: a tweak of saffron with shellfish, a splash of sherry vinegar with chicken, a scratch or two of orange zest with fish (see the mackerel recipe on page 194) are all common embellishments in my kitchen. You can swap the traditional almonds for hazelnuts, pine nuts or walnuts if you like, but I prefer almonds.

I almost always add picada late, usually to serve, as it brings the top end to herbs added earlier in cooking – a layering of flavours I love – but with briefly cooked fish, it works so well added as the fish goes into the oven.

Some swear this should be made using a mortar and pestle, but I prefer a processor.

Makes a small jarful

75g (2½oz) skinned whole almonds, roughly chopped

2 tbsp olive oil

4 slices of crusty white bread, crusts off and torn into 2.5cm (1in) pieces

2 garlic cloves, thinly sliced

small bunch of parsley, roughly chopped

sea salt and freshly ground black pepper

Toast the almonds for 2 minutes in a frying pan over a medium heat then put to one side to cool. Heat the olive oil in the same frying pan and fry the bread for about 3 minutes until crisp and golden.

Use a food processor to pulse the almonds, fried bread, garlic and parsley into a rough crumb, then season to taste.

Keeps in the fridge for a day or two.

ZA'ATAR

Depending on your threshold for authenticity, you may be frustrated in searching for the one true herb at the heart of za'atar. Hyssop, wild oregano and savory are among the prime suspects; all create a wonderful version of this classic blend. I usually go with the lightly citrus zing of Mexican oregano in summer, and hyssop or winter savory in the colder months. As with chaat masala, once you start making and using this, you'll find yourself sprinkling it on everything from oily flatbreads to eggs on toast.

Makes a small jarful

3 tbsp sesame seeds

1 ½ tbsp ground cumin

2 tbsp sumac

2 tbsp dried Mexican oregano, dried marjoram, oregano, savory or hyssop

1 tbsp salt

Lightly toast the sesame seeds in a pan over a medium heat, shuffling them around a bit to ensure they don't turn too dark. Combine all the ingredients together with a mortar and pestle, as much as anything to encourage the flavours and scents to be released as they mix.

Store in a sealed jar, where it will keep for a few months, losing intensity over time.

PERSILLADE

Persillade is really the DNA of herb combinations, double-helixing its way through so many fine sauces, mixes and dressings. It is nothing more than two marvellous ingredients with a little seasoning, but then so is gin and tonic.

Somehow, parsley and garlic chopped together, leaching their qualities into the other, creates an utterly elevating alloy beyond its simple parts. From there, the zest of a lemon creates gremolata (see below); adding lemon juice/vinegar and olive oil gives you a basic salsa verde.

Let's not get too diverted by possibilities though; in its glorious simplicity, persillade is a wonder, lending mellow depth added early, or bright elevation scattered late on a dish, as in the ox cheek braise on page 224. Try it on the deep-fried potatoes (page 137) instead of the rosemary butter, in a classic French combination.

Makes 8–10 tbsp
½ small bunch of flat-leaf parsley
1 garlic clove
sea salt and freshly ground black pepper

Finely chop the parsley and garlic together, season a little.

Gremolata
Add the zest of an unwaxed lemon to the combination above. Scatter over hot, just-fried prawns and eat with fingers and a glass of the coldest of white wines.

HERBES DE PROVENCE

As a kid, the only herbs I had experience of were in a jar of mixed herbs, that despite being used every week when Dad made bolognese, managed to reach their second decade past the sell-by date without being exhausted. It was as if once done making shoes in the night, the elves refilled that jar so we never went without. It's fair to say that all those herbs did for the dish was soak up some liquid, like so much sawdust.

This classic blend of sun-loving herbs is quite different, and part of what makes southern France southern France. I use it most when barbecuing meat and at the base of soups and stews. Adapt it to what you have – it is the spirit of it that counts more than exact quantities of specific herbs, but that is not to say you should just throw things together. The balance of resinous to bright to floral flavours is key, so experiment around this, tasting and smelling as you go.

One last thing: it is perfectly usual for me to not have dried rosemary or savory, but to have both fresh, so I add them to the mix when I'm about to use them.

Makes a small jarful

4 tbsp dried thyme

3 tbsp dried basil

1 tbsp dried oregano/marjoram

1 tbsp dried rosemary

1 tbsp dried tarragon

1 tbsp dried summer savory

1 tbsp fennel seeds

1 tbsp dried mint

1 bay leaf, whizzed into small pieces

1 tsp dried lavender

Mix everything together well in a bowl and store in a sealed container.

FINES HERBES

A classic herb combination that is one of the cornerstones of French cookery. Where herbes de Provence bring depth, fines herbes bring light. This is for where delicacy can shine: with eggs (a fines herbes omelette is special), fish, with mussels and added on serving to soups and so on.

This is one that needs no variation nor embellishment; just equal amounts of these classic herbs.

Equal amounts of:
fresh parsley
fresh chervil
fresh tarragon
fresh chives

Finely chop all your herbs together and use straight away. Simple.

PARSLEY HONEY

This is an old, slightly peculiar idea. Essentially, you simmer parsley in water, add sugar and lemon and lo, it is supposed to taste like honey. You may argue that you could simmer your old walking socks and throw that much sugar at the resulting juice and it'd taste like honey, but that's beside the point. It is superb. To my mind, it's right between an excellent intense honey and apricot jam.

I've been meaning to try this with tarragon and lovage too, but the days run away like Bukowski's wild horses over the hills.

The exact amounts here are dependent on many things, but to make a reasonable jarful use 50g (2oz) of parsley to 1.5 litres (2½ pints) or so of water, and expect to add around 500g (1lb 2oz) of sugar to the reduced parsley water.

parsley
granulated sugar
lemons

Get your jar(s) ready – sterilized and dry.

Place the parsley in a pan and cover with water (see above). Bring to the boil and simmer for 30 minutes, then strain through a sieve. To each 500ml (18fl oz) of liquid, add 500g (1lb 2oz) sugar and the juice of 2 lemons.

Boil until it thickens noticeably then jar; you can continue until it reaches the setting point (use a preserving thermometer – it should reach 105°C/220°F) if you fancy something jam-like, but I prefer it runnier, and more honey-like.

I have a small half-used jar of the first batch I made, kept out of the fridge to see how long it would last: six months and counting.

SNAIL BUTTER

As with the mole verde (page 220), no garden pests died in the making of this: it's just the butter you might put on French-style snails. It's basically garlic butter dressed up for a night out, and you can use it anywhere that suits; I love it on hot cross buns but don't tell anyone. The chives are irreplaceable here, so if you want to tweak try a touch of aniseed via chervil, tarragon or sweet cicely, or Pernod in place of the wine.

Makes about 200g (7oz)

2 garlic cloves, finely chopped

125g (4½oz) unsalted butter, softened

2 tbsp white wine or dry vermouth

4 tbsp very finely chopped chives

small bunch of flat-leaf parsley, leaves picked and very finely chopped

30g (1oz) Parma ham or prosciutto, very finely chopped (optional)

sea salt and freshly ground black pepper

Use a heavy knife to mash the garlic to a paste with a big pinch of salt. Beat together the butter and garlic paste with a wooden spoon or with an electric mixer until combined well. Beat in the wine until well combined, stir through the herbs and ham (if using), then add salt and pepper to taste.

Keeps for a week in the fridge.

TARRAGON AND PARSLEY OIL

Herb oils are especially handy in two ways; in using up a glut, and in providing an easy means of delivering herbiness in liquid form. As the base for a dressing, a drizzle on the leek tart (page 182) or a pizza, oils come into their own. You can make this with just tarragon by doubling its quantity but I like the way the parsley anchors it, making less of the tarragon seem more apparent somehow.

Makes 200ml (7fl oz)

20g (¾oz) tarragon leaves

20g (¾oz) flat-leaf parsley leaves

200ml (7fl oz) extra virgin olive oil

fine grain sea salt

Bring a pan of salted water to the boil. Blanch the herbs for just 10 seconds or so, then plunge the leaves into cold water and drain, using kitchen paper to dry them as well as you can.

Blend to a purée with the oil until entirely smooth. Strain through the finest sieve you have. Funnel the herb oil into a sterilized jar. It will keep for a few weeks in the fridge, but ideally allow it to come to room temperature before using.

DRIED FIG LEAVES

Fig leaves promise little before being toasted in a warm oven, when a fragrance fills the kitchen and intensifies in the leaf itself. It's a peculiar scent and flavour: coconut, but also much from my childhood – Shredded Wheat, popcorn and candy floss. Lay the leaves on a baking sheet, otherwise they'll cling like a school-refusing koala to the bars of the shelf as they dry.

Place the baking sheet with leaves in a single layer in a 130°C/250°F/gas mark 1 oven for as long as it takes for them to curl at the fingertips until they resemble green poppadoms, their veins coppered in the heat.

Once like this they are ready to become part of a trifle (page 245), turn up in a rice pudding (page 229) or create the wonderful syrup below, which is great in cocktails (page 262), or poured over a cake.

The dried leaves will keep for months in a sealed container, but their flavour is most intense during the first month.

FIG LEAF SYRUP

Dried fig leaves take to infusions beautifully, and this is one of my favourite syrups, great poured over cakes and ice cream, and in the pina colada mojito (page 262).

Makes about 750ml (1½ pints)

500g (1lb 2oz) caster (superfine) sugar

3 dried fig leaves (see above)

Place the sugar in a medium-sized pan with 500ml (18fl oz) water and bring to a simmer, stirring to dissolve the sugar. Remove from the heat, add the fig leaves and allow to infuse. Taste using a teaspoon, and when the strength is as you'd like it, remove the leaves. Store in a sterilized jar or bottle.

LANCASHIRE LOVAGE

This is an old, excellent way with lovage, one I learned from Nikki Duffy when taking the photographs for her River Cottage *Herb Handbook*. This works especially well with a pale crumbly cheese – the chalky Lancashire of my childhood holidays is my favourite.

Lancashire or other crumbly cheese

Lovage leaves (enough to cover the cheese)

Wrap the cheese completely in dry lovage leaves and place the whole, wrapped cheese in greaseproof paper. Store in the fridge for a week before eating for the lovage flavour to inveigle itself into the cheese.

CHIVE FLOWER VINEGAR

When does a recipe become a recipe? Perhaps we need two ingredients; 'apple' really would be testing the boundaries a touch. In any event, as bare as this is, it is excellent in its delicious simplicity. Take the flowers out when the vinegar has reached a strength of flavour you fancy, but leave it at least until the vinegar has stolen the flowers' pink ink.

You need only stick to the spirit of these quantities; I just measured what I'd done when making the last batch by eye. A vinaigrette using this is fairly hard to beat on a salad of mustardy leaves or a plainer lettuce.

Makes 325ml (11fl oz)
9 chive flowers
325ml (11fl oz) white wine vinegar

You don't need instructions, now, do you?

SALAD BURNET VINEGAR

With its succession of saw-edged oval leaves dotted along each stem and its collection of tiny crimson flowers, salad burnet is a beautiful herb. The soft young leaves bring a flush of cool cucumber flavour in leafy salads, when infused in a jug of water, a jar of gin, or here, in this clean, fresh vinegar. Sterilize the jar before use. (Pictured opposite.)

Makes 500ml (18fl oz)
12 sprigs of salad burnet
500ml (18fl oz) white wine vinegar

Jar, herb, vinegar.

TARRAGON VINEGAR

Sometimes, as with *Astral Weeks*, *The Third Man*, or tarragon vinegar, everyone bangs on about something for a very good reason. The soft, milky aniseed of tarragon in vinegar will never disappoint. Unlike some vinegars, this is best left for a week, perhaps a fortnight, before you get stuck in: taste it after seven days and see how you like it. Black peppercorns are very good here, white even better, and Szechuan just perfect. The sweetness of Mexican tarragon makes a wonderful variation if you are looking for a touch more boldness.

Makes 500ml (18fl oz)
500ml (18fl oz) white wine vinegar
6 large sprigs of French tarragon
6 peppercorns (see above)

Pour the vinegar into a tall jar or bottle, add the tarragon and the peppercorns, seal and allow to infuse. Pull out the tarragon when it is the flavour you like – it can become a little stale-tasting if left too long.

Store in a cupboard – somewhere cool and away from light.

SMALL THINGS, SOUPS AND SIDES

GREEN GAZPACHO

This is as refreshing as a fine, windless rain on a warm day. It's quick, adaptable and delicious, and if you have the sort of blender that could turn a penguin's patella into snuff in a second, you don't even have to head-start the ingredients by chopping.

While the syrup used adds a little nip of sweetness, it needn't be sage; almond or fig leaf syrup are equally wonderful.

If you are without Korean mint, go with a leaf that implies sweetness in its aniseed: sweet cicely and chervil are wonderful substitutes, or use a combination of mint and fennel leaves for a brighter result.

Serves 4

50g (2oz) crustless ciabatta, or another similar bread, cut into pieces

1 small onion, very finely chopped

2 large cucumbers, peeled and deseeded

200g (7oz) green grapes, halved, plus 50g (2oz) grapes, quartered, to garnish

60g (2¼oz) flaked (slivered) almonds, lightly toasted, plus more to garnish

150ml (5fl oz) very cold water

3 large leaves of Korean mint, finely shredded

4 tbsp extra virgin olive oil

2 tbsp sherry vinegar

2 tsp sage syrup (page 34)

1 Korean mint flower, broken into florets

sea salt and freshly ground pepper

Soak the bread in water for 5 minutes, then squeeze dry. Lightly salt the chopped onion in a bowl and rub with your fingers, then allow to rest for 10 minutes. Remove the onion from the bowl and squeeze the juice from them back into the bowl. Keep a couple of tablespoons or so of the onion and discard the rest, keeping the juice.

Roughly chop 1½ cucumbers (finely dice the remaining half and set aside for the garnish) and blitz in a blender with the grapes, almonds, bread, measured water, onion juice and half of the Korean mint leaves. Add the olive oil in a thin stream until fully emulsified. Taste and season with salt, pepper and the vinegar.

Spoon into bowls, topping with the reserved onion, grapes, cucumber, almonds and the remaining Korean mint. Drizzle with the syrup and mint flower florets and serve.

LETTUCE, ADJIKA AND SUMAC SOUP

Often as not, I'll make this on a Monday following a roast chicken Sunday. At breakfast, I'll pop the carcass in a large pan of scarcely bubbling water, with a roughly chopped leek, a carrot or two, and three bay leaves, returning in the fruitless mid-morning search for chocolate to turn it off after a couple of hours. When cool, I pick the meat and discard the bones and skin: the old man could leave a chicken like it had been through the washing machine, and I think of him every time I do this.

This soup is all about layers, building flavours, tiers of distinct interlocking deliciousness; homemade stock makes a difference to that, but shop-bought will do when life takes over. Vegetable stock will work perfectly well too.

This suits sunny days and grey.

Serves 4

1.2 litres (2¼ pints) stock

3 tbsp olive oil

2 garlic cloves, chopped

3 tbsp dried epazote (or oregano)

2 large lettuces, roughly chopped

160g (5½oz) frozen peas

a handful or two of cooked chicken, chopped into smallish pieces (optional)

8–12 tbsp adjika (page 96)

za'atar, to taste (page 110)

Warm the stock to just below a simmer. In a large pan, warm the oil over a medium heat, add the garlic and epazote and cook until the garlic is just shy of browning.

Add the lettuce and 500ml (18fl oz) of warm stock, bringing it to a simmer. Add the peas and the remaining stock and return to a gentle simmer. Cook for 10 minutes.

Use a jug to decant the chunky soup to a blender and whizz until hinting at smoothness but with smallish pieces still visible. You may need to blend in instalments, in which case use the now-empty stock pan as the holding place for the blended soup. Once complete, add all the blended soup to the large pan and bring to a simmer. Add the chicken (if using). When warmed through and ready to serve, transfer a couple of ladlefuls of soup to a jug and stir in 8 tablespoons of adjika; pour this into the soup, stirring to incorporate it throughout. Add more tablespoons to taste, if you fancy.

Ladle into bowls and sprinkle with za'atar.

HAM AND PARSLEY

I left home for an idle life with friends in a house on the bank of the Exe estuary. It remains, despite considerable competition, the laziest period of my life. We hadn't a clue about food. We lived on packet curries and dried chow meins. Occasionally, I would splash out on a packet of cod in parsley sauce and I fear I would find it as delicious now as I did then. A mile away from those boil-in-the-bags as this may be, it takes me back to discovering that glorious coming together of white sauce and parsley.

You can use flat-leaf parsley but this recipe is made for the irony depth of curly. This is somewhere between a soup and a stew; add more or less liquid as you like.

Serves 4

2 unsmoked ham hocks

2 carrots, peeled

3 celery sticks

2 onions, quartered

20 black or white peppercorns

2 bay leaves

300ml (10fl oz) whole milk

big bunch of curly parsley, stalks separated and reserved, leaves very finely chopped

40g (1½oz) butter

40g (1½oz) plain (all purpose) flour

50ml (2fl oz) double (heavy) cream (optional)

sea salt and freshly ground black pepper

boiled potatoes or mash and mustard, to serve

Soak the hocks for about 4–8 hours in the fridge (overnight is good), changing the water once or twice. Put the hocks into a large pan, cover with cold water and bring to the boil. Skim any scum off the surface and add the carrots, celery, onions, peppercorns and bay leaves and simmer gently for 2–3 hours until the meat is coming away from the bone.

When the ham is cooked take 300ml (10fl oz) of the cooking liquid (reserve the rest as a great stock) and put into a pan with the milk and the parsley stalks. Bring to the boil, remove from the heat and infuse for 15–30 minutes, then strain and keep warm.

Melt the butter in a separate pan and whisk in the flour, then cook for a minute or so until it bubbles without colouring. Gradually whisk in the infused milk, whisking until smooth before you add more, until it's all added, then simmer for about 5 minutes, stirring all the time until the sauce is thick. Stir in the chopped parsley leaves and cook for a few minutes. Check the seasoning, adding salt and pepper to taste and the cream if you'd like to enrich the sauce. Cover to keep warm.

Remove and discard the fat from the hocks and cut the meat into large chunks or shred, then rewarm in the remaining ham stock. Serve the ham with the parsley sauce and boiled potatoes or mash and mustard.

PISTOU SOUP

Minestrone is a marvellous thing. Like Mr Benn, it adopts a new identity when dressed in different clothes; in this case the clothes are pistou, and the name change reflects the happy marriage. If you prefer, a handful of chopped herbs will do a differently excellent job to serve, but I love the oiliness of this. Feel free to swap out the peas, beans and courgettes for whatever's good, cheap and in season: this should taste like a bowlful of the month you are eating it in.

Serves 4

120g (4oz) orzo pasta or any little pasta shape

4 tbsp extra virgin olive oil, plus more to coat the pasta

1 onion, finely diced

1 small leek, finely diced

2 fat celery sticks, finely diced

2 medium carrots, finely diced

2 garlic cloves, finely diced

900ml (1½ pints) hot chicken or vegetable stock

200g (7oz) peas

200g (7oz) green beans, cut into 2cm (¾in) pieces

200g (7oz) courgette (zucchini), deseeded and finely chopped

100g (3½oz) well-washed and drained spinach or chard, blanched, squeezed dry and cut into ribbons

sea salt and freshly ground black pepper

4 heaped tbsp pistou (page 94), to serve

Simmer the orzo following the instructions on the packet until al dente. Drain and rinse with cold water and coat with a little oil to prevent the pasta from clumping together.

Heat the olive oil in a large pan and sauté the onion, leek, celery and carrot for about 10–15 minutes until melting and soft but not colouring.

Add the garlic and cook for a minute with a little salt and pepper, then add the hot chicken or vegetable stock and bring to the boil, add all the green vegetables and cook for 5–8 minutes until they are just tender, then stir in the cooked orzo.

Taste and season accordingly with additional salt and pepper, then serve in bowls with a big spoonful of the pistou.

PESTO, POTATO AND GREEN BEANS

If you look at Lake Como in Italy on a map, it resembles a skinny blue figure, striding west through the hills of northern Italy. When I was younger and less unpleasant to look at, I sat in the crotch of that figure, able to see north into its watery torso, and southwest and southeast along each of its blue legs. It was a good day. I ate pasta pesto, alone, with a little too much lunchtime wine in the autumn sun. It remains the only time I can say that pasta with pesto has made me happy – I much prefer it with vegetables of all kinds, and perhaps nowhere more so than in this. Don't let its simplicity fool you; this is special.

Serves 4

800g (1lb 12oz) new potatoes, peeled and cut into even sized pieces

500g (1lb 2oz) runner beans, trimmed and sliced (use green beans if you prefer)

¾ batch of pesto (page 98)

Cook the potatoes in plenty of boiling salted water for about 15 minutes until tender, adding the beans for the final 5 minutes of cooking time. Remove from the heat, drain and keep warm.

Toss the pesto (more or less as you like) with the warm potatoes and beans and serve warm.

DEEP-FRIED POTATOES IN ROSEMARY BUTTER

There are good ideas and there are Good Ideas, and this is very definitely a Good Idea. You are never too full to eat a skipful of these. You need a deep-fat fryer or a fairly accurate temperature probe, and do cut the potatoes to the same size to ensure they cook evenly.

Serves 4

1 garlic clove, crushed to a paste with a little salt

1 tbsp finely chopped fresh rosemary

½ tsp freshly cracked black pepper

60g (2¼oz) butter, softened

1kg (2lb 4oz) floury potatoes, cut into 2cm (¾in) dice (I leave the skin on)

oil, for deep-frying

flaky sea salt, to serve

Work the garlic, rosemary and pepper into the butter, then pop into the fridge. Once firm, cut into 6 pieces and return to the fridge.

Put the potatoes into a pan and rinse until the water runs clear, then fill with clean water. Bring to the boil, spooning away any foam rising to the surface, then lower the heat to a simmer and cook for 3 minutes. Turn off the heat and use a slotted spoon to lift the potatoes into a colander, then on to a large flat baking sheet in a single layer to cool completely, while also drying out.

Fill a deep-fat fryer or a large pan (no more than a third full) with oil and heat to 110°C/230°F for the first fry. Place a large flat dish beside the fryer, lined with kitchen paper. Cook the potatoes in batches until pale and tender. Lift from the oil with a slotted spoon, allowing as much oil to drip back into the pan as possible, then lay on the paper in a single layer.

Increase the oil temperature to 180°C/350°F and fry the potatoes again until very crisp and golden. Use the slotted spoon to lift them from the oil to the kitchen paper, then into a bowl. Immediately toss through the butter until melted and absorbed, sprinkle generously with salt and serve straight away.

HERB TEMPURA

It's quite hard to find many things that when submerged into hot fat and dusted with salt aren't deeply pleasing to eat. Tempura is that perfect blend of completely addictive and insubstantial, meaning you can keep adding more to the pan in the vain attempt to satisfy your desire for more.

One thing is crucial: mix the ingredients quickly together, like you don't really mean it, to avoid getting the flour's gluten going. Lumps are fine; the batter should – like a dress at Cannes – just cling here and there.

Wild garlic flowers and the bolder herbs are the ones to go for: coriander, sage, lemon verbena, parsley and chives are especially good.

A sharp chilli-tamarind dip is very good to go with.

Serves 4 as a snack (or 1 greedy pig)

400ml (14fl oz) groundnut oil

75g (2½oz) cornflour (cornstarch)

75g (2½oz) plain (all purpose) flour

1 tsp salt

1 egg yolk

150ml (5fl oz) sparkling water

small sprigs of herbs of your choice (see above)

flaky sea salt, to serve

Over a medium heat, warm the oil in a medium pan (the oil should come about one-third up the sides). When a cube of bread sizzles to a quick copper, you can fry your battered herbs.

Quickly mix the flours, salt, egg yolk and sparkling water together in a large bowl to form a batter; don't worry about any lumps.

Dip the herb into the batter and lower carefully into the hot oil. Expect patchy batter coverage; it is as it should be. Ninety seconds should be enough to fry them perfectly. Fish out on to kitchen paper, using a slotted spoon. Shower with salt and eat in a hurry.

ROSEMARY AND BASIL AUBERGINES IN ZA'ATAR

This is my favourite way with aubergines, and one that shows how they take beautifully to so many herbs. The oregano in the za'atar and the rosemary lend flavour to the cooking aubergines, while the fresh basil scattered to serve completes the picture. Adding the rosemary for the last few minutes aromatizes the aubergines; I know 'aromatize' sounds like the sort of unwelcome thing a garage unexpectedly does to your car when you've taken it for an MOT, but I promise it is the best word for it. It is as if resinous smoke has been blown through every pore of the aubergine, without a trace of the bitterness that comes with roasting rosemary sprigs until they resemble the skeletons of sparrows' legs. Try this with roast lamb, griddled courgettes, couscous and pretty much any cold cuts.

Serves 4

4 aubergines (eggplant), quartered lengthways

4 tbsp olive oil

a few good sprigs of rosemary, broken into 3cm (1in) pieces

4 tbsp za'atar (page 110)

sea salt and freshly ground black pepper

For the dressing

50g (2oz) tahini

1 tbsp yoghurt

juice of 1 lemon

2 garlic cloves, finely chopped

2 tbsp olive oil

To serve

pomegranate molasses

hot sauce or chilli flakes

handful of Greek basil leaves, or other basil finely shredded

Preheat the oven to 200°C/400°F/gas mark 6.

Lay the aubergine quarters in a single layer on baking sheets, brush with oil, and sprinkle with salt and pepper. Place in the oven, turn the heat down to 180°C/350°F/gas mark 4, and cook for 20–25 minutes until tender and brown.

Make the dressing by whisking all the ingredients together with 2 tablespoons water; use a little more water if required, to reach a consistency of double (heavy) cream.

Mix the rosemary, za'atar and a heavy grinding of pepper in a bowl. Remove the aubergines from the oven, top with the za'atar mix, drizzle with more oil and return to the oven for 5 minutes.

Drizzle with the tahini dressing, pomegranate molasses, hot sauce or chilli flakes and scatter with basil.

ZA'ATAR FLATBREADS

These easy flatbreads, pebble-dashed with the herby zing of za'atar, make pretty much any soup a more joyous prospect; a fattoush wouldn't be half as fine without them (page 175).

Makes 8

2 tsp active dry yeast

4 tbsp olive oil

350ml (12fl oz) warm water

500g (1lb 2oz) bread flour, plus a little more for rolling

½ tsp salt

2 tbsp za'atar (page 110)

Add the yeast and 2 tablespoons of the olive oil to the water and stir until the yeast is dissolved.

Mix this into the flour in a large bowl until completely combined. Cover and leave for 10 minutes to rest. Fold the salt in with your hands then cover and rest for 10 minutes more.

Stretch and fold the dough, turning the dough 90 degrees and repeating 7 times, then cover and allow to stand in a warm place for at least 30 minutes, ideally an hour.

Divide the dough into 8 pieces, then roll out into ovals about 5mm (¼in) thick.

In batches, cook the flatbreads in a hot, dry frying pan for 2 minutes until puffed up and slightly charred, then flip over and cook the other side until slightly charred. Brush with the remaining olive oil, and sprinkle with za'atar. Eat as soon as possible.

REFRIED BEANS

My daughter loves refried beans, especially in a tortilla, burritos or as a dip with tortilla chips, and this is the way I like to cook them. This is also special smeared on toast (heresy!), or with rice and cucumber/tomato/onion salads. Most often I use tinned beans, though dried/soaked are just that bit better if you have time to do them ahead. Bay and epazote lay the herb foundations here – epazote is a classic herb in refried beans – with oregano joining the party after a few drinks. Mexican oregano works really well, with its lemony edge.

Serves 4

250g (9oz) dried black beans, soaked in cold water overnight or throughout the day

3 bay leaves

2 tsp epazote

6 tbsp olive oil

1 onion, finely chopped

1 green pepper, finely chopped

3 garlic cloves, finely chopped

1 tsp ground cumin

1 tsp fresh oregano (dried will do)

sea salt and freshly ground black pepper

Drain the soaked beans, rinse and put in a large deep pan with enough fresh cold water to cover the beans by at least 5cm (2in). Bring to the boil and skim off any froth that appears on the surface. Add the bay and epazote and simmer, half-covered for 1½–2 hours until the beans are tender. Top up with boiling water if needed.

While the beans cook, heat half the olive oil in a large pan, add the onion and pepper and cook over a medium heat for 8–10 minutes until soft. Add the garlic, cumin, oregano, 1 teaspoon salt and a good grinding of black pepper and cook for 1 minute, then remove from the heat.

Once cooked, drain the beans, reserving the cooking liquid. Add the beans to the onion mix, stirring and mashing to combine, adding spoonfuls of the cooking liquid until you reach the desired consistency – nicely pourable. Whizz a third in a blender, then stir into the rest, tasting and seasoning with salt and pepper if needed.

Warm the remaining olive oil in a frying pan over a moderately high heat. Add the bean mixture and cook, stirring frequently, for 5 minutes or so, until it has thickened just a touch to barely pourable.

HERB SODA BREAD

Get breakfast right and the day has every chance of going your way. When the fridge and cupboards are bereft of excellent food, the hassle of shopping or kneading can be dodged with this smasher of a recipe. Soda bread sits (ideally, for breakfast) right between the savoury and the sweet. It is perfectly neither. A few minutes of bringing together ingredients you are very likely to have to hand gives you 40 minutes or so to walk the dog, make sweet lurve or indeed to sneak somewhere quiet and enjoy a coffee without being mithered. Many herbs (though for heaven's sake don't try mint) work well here: chives, sweet cicely and either of the savories are especially good.

Makes 2 medium loaves

good handful of oats

700g (1½lb) white flour, plus extra for dusting

50g (2oz) wholemeal flour

1½ tsp salt

15g (½oz) bicarbonate of soda (baking soda)

600ml (1 pint) buttermilk (or milk with 2 tbsp lemon juice)

small bunch of chives or sweet cicely, etc., finely chopped

Preheat the oven 200°C/400°F/gas mark 6.

Scatter a few oats on a baking sheet. Sift both flours into a wide bowl with the salt and bicarb. Make a well in the centre and pour the buttermilk in gradually, tip in the fresh herbs and use your hand or a wooden spoon to gently mix in. Don't mix it too much, just enough to form a sticky cohesive dough.

Lightly flour a work surface and tip the dough on to it. Separate into 2 and form into rounds. Slash the top of each with a deep X and place on the baking sheet. Sprinkle a few oats over the top and bake for 35–45 minutes until well risen and nicely coloured – the undersides should sound hollow when they're done. Transfer to a wire rack and ideally eat warm.

TARRAGON RÉMOULADE

Rémoulade: now there's a name for a self-important prog rock covers band. It is also one of my favourite sides, simple as it is – which is, essentially, posh coleslaw. It's so good with ham, a grilled oily fish, or as one of a number of sides to pretty much anything.

Make it near to serving as it can get a little gloopy after an hour or two, thanks to the crème fraîche. Deviate at will: kohlrabi instead of (or as well as) the celeriac, and a few nigella or black mustard seeds work really well. A little lovage, a few leaves of Korean mint, sweet cicely or fenugreek leaves are excellent variations.

Serves 4

1 celeriac (about 700g/1½lb), peeled and cut into matchsticks or coarsely grated

juice of 1 lemon

200g (7oz) crème fraîche

2 tbsp Dijon mustard

a few good sprigs of tarragon, leaves only, finely chopped

sea salt and freshly ground black pepper

As soon as it is cut, tumble the celeriac through half the lemon juice in a bowl to stop it discolouring.

In another bowl, mix the remaining lemon juice, crème fraîche, mustard, half the tarragon and seasoning together. Stir the dressing into the celeriac, sprinkle over the remaining tarragon, and serve.

METHI PARATHA

Possibly my favourite flatbread, though in fairness that's what I think when I'm eating pretty much any flatbread. The fenugreek leaf (aka methi) is the single herbal presence here, infusing the dough as it cooks. I haven't found a curry (or indeed a soup) that this doesn't accompany beautifully.

Makes 4 (or 6–8 smaller ones)

400g (14oz) strong bread flour, plus extra for dusting

100g (3½oz) wholemeal flour

½ tsp caster (superfine) sugar

1 tsp salt

300ml (10fl oz) water

small bunch of fenugreek leaf, finely chopped (or use 1 tbsp dried fenugreek)

40g (1½oz) ghee or butter, melted

good pinch of ajwain or garam masala

Mix both flours with the sugar, salt and water and bring it together into a soft dough. Cover and put to one side for 5 minutes, then knead for a couple of minutes until smooth. Cover well and put to one side for 10 minutes.

Stir a couple of tablespoons of chopped fenugreek leaf into the melted ghee or butter.

Divide the dough into 4 and on a floured surface roll each piece into a ball, then each ball into a circle about 15cm (6in) in diameter. Brush each with a teaspoon of ghee and sprinkle over some more fenugreek and a little pinch of ajwain or garam masala. Roll each up (with the oil on the inside) to a cigar shape, then coil up into a snail. Press down with the palm of your hand and roll them again to a circle about 15cm (6in) in diameter.

Dry fry in small batches in a hot pan until beginning to char, then flip over and cook the other side. Place in a bowl covered with a clean cloth while you repeat with the rest of the paratha. Give each a little brush of ghee and scatter with the remaining fenugreek to serve.

PANI PURI AND GREEN CHUTNEY

Here, an attempt to recreate a special Indian street food, where puris – crisp, hollow globes – are filled with a chickpea salad and the liveliest of green chutneys. Eaten in one, like a spicy shot, the explosion of flavour in your mouth is really something.

I'm going to advise you against making your own puris. There is quite the art to making those spherical shells; they should puff up but are often reluctant, though they are perfectly delicious as crisp discs.

Should you wish to try, mix 200g (7oz) semolina, 2 tablespoons flour, ¼ teaspoon bicarbonate of soda (baking soda) and a generous pinch of salt in a bowl and slowly add 125ml (4fl oz) soda water, bringing everything together in a dough, and allow it to rest for half an hour. Roll it into a sausage, cut 1cm (½in) coins of dough from it, rolling them into thin, flat circles around 6cm (2½in) across. Deep-fry in sunflower oil for 4 minutes or so, until golden, flipping them over halfway through. Drain on kitchen paper.

You could, of course, use mini poppadoms instead of puri shells.

If you have my previous book, *Sour*, you'll notice that the filling is similar to chana chaat salad, but this is a very different experience.

Makes 24

bunch of coriander (cilantro), roughly chopped

200g (7oz) cooked chickpeas (garbanzos), drained

½ cucumber, peeled, halved, deseeded and very finely chopped

2 tomatoes, very finely chopped

1 small red onion, very finely chopped

24 pani puri shells

one batch of Indian green chutney (page 92)

sea salt and freshly ground black pepper

To serve

yoghurt (optional)

sev or Bombay mix (optional)

In a bowl, stir together the coriander, chickpeas, cucumber, tomatoes and red onion, and add salt and pepper to taste. Pop a hole into the top of each pani, and fill with a teaspoon of the chickpea mix, add another of green chutney and, if you fancy, a drizzle of yoghurt and a sprinkle of sev or Bombay mix. Eat immediately.

BIGGER THINGS

HERBY EGG MAYO ON TOAST

When I was very small, I used to talk to God. I'd ask only small things of him as he didn't seem too keen to get on with significant matters like world peace and keeping Brotherhood of Man from Number 1. I asked that he make sure Clive Lloyd scored a century, that the cat wouldn't get run over, and that I didn't misbehave and thereby miss out on the huge lolly I'd been promised at the carnival. Eventually, I lost the belief – I'm not sure I ever had it – but if we still talked, I would ask (given that world peace still seems a long shot) that everyone ate one thing a day that gave them as much pleasure as this gives me. And yes, the cat did get run over. But I got the lolly. You win some…

Serves 2

6 medium eggs

9 tbsp mayo (about 150g/5oz)

1 small shallot, very finely chopped

2 tbsp each of finely chopped tarragon, chives, parsley

4 slices of your favourite toast

chive flowers (optional)

olive oil, for drizzling

sea salt and freshly ground black pepper

Boil the eggs to your preference: personally, for this, I like them so that they'd equally piss off those who normally like a runny yolk, and those who like it set. For the merest hint of mercury-like movement in the yellow, lower the eggs into boiling water and simmer for 7 minutes. Drain and run under cold water to cool the shells.

Peel and coarsely grate or roughly chop the eggs. Mix in the mayo, shallot and chopped herbs (reserving a tablespoon or so to sprinkle), then season to taste with salt and a generous amount of pepper.

Spoon on to the toast and top with the remaining herbs, some chive flowers if you have them, and a drizzle of oil. Another grind of pepper might not go amiss.

KUKU SABZI

If you have any of my other books, you will have gathered that I do love a recipe that serves equally well as an excellent breakfast, a quick lunch or a solo dinner, and this is one of the best. Use as little or as much chilli as you like, adapt the herbs to what you have or fancy, and don't be above adding a tweak of garam masala or chaat masala.

Serves 4

4 tbsp olive oil

1 bunch of spring onions (scallions), trimmed and thinly sliced

150g (5oz) fresh herbs (use any combination of parsley, coriander/cilantro, dill, chives, mint, tarragon), leaves only, finely chopped

100g (3½oz) spinach, very thinly sliced

½ tsp ground turmeric

6 medium eggs, beaten

1 tbsp plain (all purpose) flour

½ tsp sea salt

freshly ground black pepper

To serve (optional)

2 tbsp walnuts, chopped

1 fresh green chilli, thinly sliced

Preheat the grill to medium.

Heat half the olive oil in a large frying pan and cook the spring onions for 2–3 minutes until softened, then tip the oil and onions into a large bowl. Add all the remaining ingredients to the bowl and stir to combine.

Add the remaining oil to the frying pan and place over a medium heat. Pour in the mixture, cover the pan and cook for 5 minutes over a low heat until almost set, then place under the grill (broiler) for 1–2 minutes to set the top.

Serve topped with more freshly ground black pepper, a pinch of sea salt and the walnuts and chilli (if using).

ROMAN HERB AND ANCHOVY SALAD

Pour yourself a large glass of wine and one of water and prepare to masticate. The barely chopped herbs require you to chew, to properly chew in a way that we rarely do: the reward of it being your teeth rather than the knife that turn the herbs into something you can swallow is the most extraordinary flavour. You may well feel that you have never tasted chervil and parsley so completely.

Classically, this sort of salad might be dominated by puntarelle but the celery and herbs work so very well here. You can use any bitter leaves, such as chicory, dandelion, endive, escarole and radicchio, and even mustard leaf, watercress or rocket if you prefer.

Serves 4 as a starter

2 tbsp capers, rinsed, drained and chopped

12 anchovies, drained and roughly chopped

finely grated zest and juice of 1 unwaxed lemon

1 garlic clove, finely chopped

2 tbsp red wine vinegar

½ tsp chilli flakes, or more to taste

6 tbsp extra virgin olive oil

6 tbsp coarse breadcrumbs

leaves and stalks from 1 celery heart, thinly sliced

big bunch of chervil, barely chopped

big bunch of parsley, barely chopped

sea salt and freshly cracked black pepper

Mix the capers, anchovies, lemon zest and juice, garlic, vinegar and chilli flakes and season to taste with salt and pepper (go easy, as it should be quite salty already). Allow to marinate for about 10 minutes, then stir through 4 tablespoons of the olive oil.

Fry the breadcrumbs in the remaining 2 tablespoons olive oil (add a squashed garlic clove and a good sprig of rosemary if you like) until golden and crisp; they keep well, so you can make a big batch.

Combine the celery and herbs with the oily anchovy mix, scatter over the breadcrumbs and serve.

FIG, GOAT'S CHEESE AND HERB SALAD

This is what can happen when you put a few complementary ingredients together, dress them simply and don't complicate matters. The three sizes of herb leaves bring different impact, with the parsley as much a salad leaf as a herb. As good on a sunny day as it is by the fire with a glass of red.

Serves 4

big handful of rocket (arugula) and/or watercress

big handful of lamb's lettuce or baby spinach

small bunch of mint, leaves shredded

small bunch of basil, leaves sliced in half

small bunch of flat-leaf parsley, leaves only

8 ripe figs, each cut into 6

40g (1½oz) walnuts, roughly chopped

4 tbsp extra virgin olive oil

2 tbsp aged red wine vinegar (or use balsamic vinegar)

150g (5oz) soft goat's cheese (or use labneh)

sea salt and freshly ground black pepper

Combine the salad leaves and herbs together in a bowl and season with salt and pepper. Lay out on a large platter or plate and top with the figs and walnuts.

Whisk together the oil and vinegar and drizzle over the leaves and figs, then dot with blobs of cheese. Serve immediately.

GRIDDLED PEACHES, BASIL, WATERCRESS, PARMESAN AND PINE NUTS

If you have an excellent peach – and by that I mean one you caught as it fell from its parent, that truly smells like a peach, or that you have acquired from the person who grew it – sit and eat it in peace. It will make you very, very happy. For any that are shy of perfection, heat works wonders. A minute of two on a furious griddle or frying pan brings sweetness, a little bitterness where it blackens, and softens the otherwise reluctant fruit. The observant will notice that this salad is one that uses the ingredients of pesto, each of which pair so well individually with peaches, and even more so in an ensemble. If you have a few varieties of basil – Greek and Thai work well here – then do include a mix. This makes a mighty fine starter or lunch.

Serves 4

4 small ripe but firm peaches, stoned, halved or quartered

extra virgin olive oil

100g (3 ½ oz) watercress

red wine vinegar or lemon juice, to taste

small bunch of basil, leaves picked (a mix of varieties is nice), and a few flowers if you have them

30g (1oz) pine nuts, lightly toasted

50g (2oz) Parmesan, shaved or coarsely grated

sea salt and freshly ground black pepper

Give the peaches a good coating of olive oil and season with salt and pepper. Place a griddle pan over a high heat and sear the peaches on each cut surface until caramelized. Place on a chopping board to cool a little.

Slice the peaches and arrange over a platter or individual plates. Toss the watercress with olive oil and vinegar or lemon juice to taste, then add to the peaches. Scatter over the basil, pine nuts and Parmesan, and finish with a good grinding of salt and pepper.

CHERRIES, LANCASHIRE LOVAGE, HONEY, LAVENDER

In the year before Big School, we spent summers in Lancashire with my cousins. Days were about catching sticklebacks in the beck, playing cricket in the field behind their house and trying to persuade parents that a Screwball ice cream in the morning and the afternoon was a good idea. I also developed a taste for Lancashire cheese that has never left me. Here, it pairs so very well with the bitter excellence of lovage and the sweet come hither of lavender. The cherries and honey seal the deal perfectly, with toast or crackers providing a little crunch to go with.

Serves 4

250g (9oz) Lancashire lovage (page 122)

good toast or crackers

about 20 cherries, stoned

a few sprigs of lavender

a little pot of runny honey

Serve the cheese in crumbly slices on toast or crackers, topped with cherries, a couple of lavender flowers and a drizzle of honey.

SPELT WITH CUCUMBER, LEMON, LOVAGE AND MINT

This is exactly the sort of thing that mid-twenties me just wouldn't have been interested in, which shows there are a great many advantages to being less young. It's halfway to a tabbouleh, and should be similarly generous on herbs. It's substantial enough to go with leafy salads, leeks mimosa (page 167) or sausages, lamb or roasted vegetables if you are looking for a larger meal.

Care in chopping is effectively an ingredient here: it will taste so much better if you do it well. A chiffonade works best, giving little bursts of flavour that a finer chop misses.

Serves 4

250g (9oz) pearled spelt

40 mint leaves

generous handful of flat-leaf parsley, most of the stalks discarded

12 medium-sized lovage leaves

1 cucumber, halved, deseeded and diced

seeds from 2 pomegranates

finely grated zest of 1 unwaxed lemon, plus the juice of ½

150ml (5fl oz) extra virgin olive oil

sea salt and freshly ground black pepper

Rinse the spelt thoroughly, place in a pan and cover with water. Bring to the boil, reduce to a simmer and cook until just firm: 20–25 minutes is usual. Drain in a sieve and allow it to release its steam for a few minutes.

To prepare the herbs, you will need the sharpest of knives. Your only job here is to avoid bruising the herbs, and to do this you need to slice through them cleanly in one pass: a keen blade and a thin layer of herbs is crucial. A chiffonade works best here (page 25). Roll half the mint leaves into a cigar and slice finely to give the thinnest filaments of mint. Repeat for the rest of the mint, the parsley and the lovage.

Put the cucumber and pomegranate seeds into a bowl, add the lemon zest, juice and olive oil and season well. Stir the herbs in, then add the spelt and stir to incorporate everything thoroughly.

Taste and adjust the seasonings if necessary. Serve immediately, warm.

LEEKS MIMOSA

When the sky is full of showers and the asparagus is growing towards them,
I make a coming together of those sweet green spears, grated egg and early
season herbs, likely as not sweet cicely and chives. It starts a cycle of similarly
seasonal lunches, where the star and the herbs that adorn it reflect what's best at
the time. Here then, leeks, but green beans, runners, garlic scapes and even sliced
courgettes substitute equally well. A good pinch of garam masala is wonderful,
but chaat masala, ras el hanout or za'atar are superb too.

Serves 4 as a starter or lunch

4 medium eggs

8 thin leeks, or 4 thick, washed well and trimmed to less than the width of a large pan

3 tbsp English mustard

2 tbsp lemon juice

1 tbsp honey

3 tbsp extra virgin olive oil

leaves from 6 tarragon stems, chopped

2 tbsp capers

3 chive flowers, broken into florets

small handful of dill, chopped

finely grated zest of 1 unwaxed lemon

a couple of good pinches of garam masala

sea salt and freshly ground black pepper

Place the eggs in a pan of cold water, bring to the boil and immediately turn
off the heat. Leave the eggs in the water for 12 minutes and then run cold
water into the pan for a minute or so to stop the cooking process.

Lower the leeks into a large pan of simmering water and cook until they take
the point of a knife – likely to be 15–25 minutes depending on their thickness.

Make the dressing in a medium bowl: whisk the mustard, lemon juice, honey
and a couple of pinches of salt together, then whisk in the olive oil.

Peel the cooled eggs and then coarsely grate them. Drain the leeks, and lay
them on a large plate or dish, then top with the grated egg. Scatter over the
tarragon, capers, the chive florets, dill and lemon zest, dust with garam
masala, season with salt and pepper, and finally splash with the dressing.

COURGETTES, GOOSEBERRIES, PEAS, SWEET CICELY, LAMB'S LETTUCE

Sweet cicely is such a crazily under-appreciated herb. You can't buy it, few grow it, yet it will happily colonize a damp, shady corner and appear early in spring to remind you that sunnier days are ahead. Its gentle aniseed flavour implies sweetness, which makes its presence alongside sharp fruit – rhubarb, classically – a fine (and potentially healthier) one. Here it works its magic on gooseberries. If you don't have sweet cicely, fennel fronds, Korean mint, Thai or Greek basil, tarragon or chervil will do something similar.

Serves 4

6 small courgettes (zucchini), halved lengthways

150g (5oz) gooseberries, topped and tailed

2 shallots, thinly sliced

olive oil, for drizzling

4 tbsp vinegar or kombucha

200g (7oz) raw shelled peas

large handful of lamb's lettuce

a few sprigs of sweet cicely

sea salt and freshly ground black pepper

Preheat the oven to 200°C/400°F/gas mark 6.

Take 2 baking sheets and place the courgettes on one and the gooseberries and shallots on another. Drizzle both with olive oil and season with salt and pepper, then splash lightly with the vinegar/kombucha. Roast the courgettes for about 5 minutes until just about tender and still firm, and the gooseberries a little longer, until they are collapsed and have released their juices. Allow both to cool.

Place the gooseberry mixture in a bowl and add a bit more oil to make a dressing. Mix the courgettes with the peas and lamb's lettuce. Season to taste with salt and pepper and place in a bowl, then top with the gooseberry dressing and sprigs of the sweet cicely.

GRAPEFRUIT, MANGO, FETA, SUGAR SNAPS, FENNEL AND DILL

Around the time 'Are Friends Electric?' knocked everyone sideways, I was eating a lot of grapefruit for breakfast. Even now, if I hear the song, I can taste that sharp juice; and if I taste a grapefruit, I can hear the song that still sounds like the future. In complete coincidence, it came on the radio when I first made this, which I take as a sign that this recipe was meant to be. Fennel and dill look mighty similar, yet their flavours couldn't be further apart. Occasionally they jar; here they are perfect partners, elevating everything to a brighter whole.

I like this quite big on the herbs but ease off if you fancy, and do serve as individual plates if you prefer.

Serves 4

2 grapefruit, peeled and thinly sliced into rounds

extra virgin olive oil, for drizzling

100g (3½oz) sugar snaps, sliced in half

2 ripe mangoes, peeled, stoned and thinly sliced

200g (7oz) feta

½ handful of fennel fronds, roughly chopped

½ handful of dill fronds, roughly chopped

small handful of pistachios, lightly crushed

good pinch of chilli flakes

sea salt and freshly ground black pepper

Lay the grapefruit on a platter and drizzle with olive oil.

Toss the sugar snaps and mango together with a little olive oil, salt (just a little; the feta is salty) and pepper and spread over the grapefruit. Crumble the feta over, sprinkle with the herbs and pistachios, then finish with the chilli flakes.

APPLE, QUARTERED CHARRED LITTLE GEMS, PANCETTA, SHISO 'ZA'ATAR'

Za'atar is a remarkable coming together of earthy/resinous cumin and oregano, with the sour brightness of sumac, salt and sesame seeds; plus it's easy to make (page 110). Here, I've taken the spirit of it and used shiso's wonderful cumin/mint flavour in place of actual cumin and oregano and it works perfectly. The sourness missing from this that Mexican oregano brings to my za'atar is balanced by using good sharp apples. When I had a couple of sweeter apples, I made this with Vietnamese coriander instead of shiso and the implied sourness of its lemon/coriander flavour worked a treat.

Serves 4

2 little gem lettuces, quartered

4 tbsp olive oil

100g (3 ½ oz) pancetta or lardons

2 tart apples

3 tbsp red wine vinegar

1 tbsp Dijon mustard (optional)

10 leaves shiso, thinly sliced if large

3 tbsp sesame seeds, toasted in a dry pan

2 tsp sumac

sea salt and freshly ground black pepper

Heat a dry frying pan over a high heat and sear the two cut sides of the little gem quarters: you're looking for quick charring while retaining crunch. Remove from the frying pan and arrange on a platter. Add the oil to the pan and cook the pancetta for about 5 minutes until golden and it has released its fat.

Meanwhile, thinly slice the apples (equatorially rather than polar), remove the seeds and scatter the slices over the lettuce. Take the pan off the heat and use a slotted spoon to lift the lardons on to the gems, keeping the oil in the pan.

Stir the vinegar and mustard into the oil in the pan and drizzle over the salad. Sprinkle the shiso, sesame seeds and sumac over the salad, and season generously with salt and pepper.

FATTOUSH

We have a 'no piggling' rule in our house – no one is allowed to plunder leftovers for their preferred bits, thereby rendering the whole less desirable – and nowhere is this more acutely observed than with fattoush. The torn za'atar flatbread pieces, glistening with dressing and tomato juice and glittered with herbs, hold everything together, but boy are they good on their own.

This is another recipe where the differently sized leaves make such an impression on the flavour; with nothing finely chopped, when you come across a piece of herb, you know it.

Mint and parsley are the classic pairing for this, but you should go where you fancy. Dill will dominate but can be good; fennel fronds bring brightness; fresh oregano or marjoram will both offer a little oily sunshine.

Serves 4

2 za'atar flatbreads (page 142) or use pitta breads dusted with za'atar or sumac

juice of 1 lemon

3 tbsp good-quality olive oil

pinch of sea salt

1 little gem lettuce, shredded

½ cucumber, peeled, halved, deseeded and thinly sliced

200g (7oz) cherry tomatoes, halved

200g (7oz) radishes, thinly sliced

big bunch of parsley, leaves picked and left whole

3 lovage leaves, shredded

1cm (½in) thick ponytail of chives, roughly chopped

6 or so mint leaves, finely shredded

Split the breads in half, then toast until they are crisp and dry. Break them into bite-sized pieces.

Make a dressing by mixing the lemon juice with the oil, and a big pinch of salt.

Mix the lettuce, cucumber, tomatoes, radishes, parsley and bread pieces together, then stir in the dressing. Scatter with the herbs and serve.

WATERMELON AND PARSLEY FATTOUSH WITH YOGHURT DRESSING

Fattoush may well be the noise a ripe watermelon makes as it hits the pavement when dropped from a crane. I hope so. I woke up one morning with the idea for this sitting right at the front of the queue of new day thoughts; here, after a few tweaks, it is.

The slightly inky scent – like a leaky Bic – of watermelon and the herbs together, gives this a strange saffronish backbeat. The parsley, whole, as a salad leaf, is so good here. Adapt as you like: white grapes, halved, instead of/with the radishes is a very fine move, as is mint in place of the chives, with dried oregano instead of the mint in the dressing.

Serves 4

2 za'atar flatbreads (page 142) or use pitta breads dusted with za'atar or sumac

finely grated zest and juice of 1 unwaxed lemon

3 tbsp good-quality olive oil

good pinch of sea salt

1 little gem lettuce, shredded

½ cucumber, peeled, halved, deseeded and thinly sliced

200g (7oz) watermelon, peeled, deseeded and cubed

200g (7oz) radishes, thinly sliced

large bunch of flat-leaf parsley, whole leaves only

3 tsp dried mint

2 garlic cloves, very finely chopped

120g (4oz) yoghurt

1cm (½in) thick ponytail of chives, roughly chopped

Split the breads in half, toast until they are crisp and dry, and break them into pieces.

Whisk the lemon juice into the oil with the salt in a large bowl, then tumble in the lettuce, cucumber, watermelon, radishes, parsley and bread pieces. Spread this out on a large platter.

Stir the lemon zest, dried mint and chopped garlic into the yoghurt and splatter over the salad. Scatter over the chives and serve.

SPICY HERB AND NOODLE SALAD

Most writers I know get by on egg on toast or leftovers for lunch – when you are on the scribble, it's good not to get out of the zone for long. This is for the other days: a bowl of lively refreshment when you are flagging. It is so very simple, yet full of flavours rubbing up against each other like passengers on a jammed tube. It has a fair bit of South East Asia about it, and I like it quite fierce on the chilli.

Serves 4

2 large garlic cloves, very finely chopped

1–3 Thai birds-eye chillies, thinly sliced

1 large shallot, very thinly sliced

1 tbsp palm sugar (or use soft light brown sugar)

2 ripe tomatoes, seeds squeezed out and juice sieved out and reserved, flesh thinly sliced

1 tbsp fish sauce

juice of 1 large lime

2 tart apples, like Granny Smith

handful of cold/barely warm cooked rice noodles

1 little gem or soft round lettuce, washed and shredded

small bunch of basil (green, purple or Thai), leaves picked

small bunch of mint, leaves picked

small bunch of coriander (cilantro), leaves picked

4 tbsp roasted cashews or peanuts, crushed to a powder

Mix together the garlic, chillies, shallot and sugar, then stir in the tomato water, fish sauce and lime juice. Taste and adjust the seasonings as you like and put to one side to infuse.

Slice or shred the apples with a peeler or cut them into matchsticks by hand, putting them straight into salted water. Drain the apple and put into a large bowl with the dressing, noodles, lettuce, sliced tomato and all the herbs. Top with the nut powder and serve immediately.

GREEK HERB PIE

This Greek summer favourite, aka spanakopita, is so worth making a delicious regular. Heavy with spinach, salty feta and crisp laminations of filo, it's as good cold as hot, early in the day as late. This version nudges the spinach (which can be a bit of a grump at times) towards the cheerful with the brightness of dill and mint in generous quantities, and parsley anchoring the leeks to the cheese. A delight.

Serves 4–6

1 onion, finely chopped

2 leeks, thinly sliced

150g (5oz) butter, melted

300g (10oz) cooked or frozen spinach, drained

200g (7oz) crumbled feta

200g (7oz) ricotta

4 medium eggs, beaten

small bunch of dill, finely chopped

small bunch of flat-leaf parsley, finely chopped

small bunch of mint, finely chopped

1 bunch of spring onions (scallions), thinly sliced

1 tsp ground cumin

1 tsp ground coriander

200g (7oz) filo pastry

1 tsp nigella seeds (or use sesame seeds)

sea salt and freshly ground black pepper

In a frying pan over a medium heat, fry the onion and the leeks in 1 tablespoon of the melted butter for 10 minutes until soft. Preheat the oven to 190°C/375°F/gas mark 5 and grease a roasting tin or baking dish with some of the butter.

Tip the softened onion and leeks into a bowl, add the spinach, feta, ricotta, eggs, herbs, spring onions, ground spices, some salt and plenty of black pepper and stir to combine.

Lay 3 sheets of filo pastry in the prepared tin, overlapping them a little and brushing each sheet with melted butter. Place the filling on top and spread out evenly. Top with the remaining sheets, buttering each layer. Generously brush the top with the remaining butter and sprinkle with the seeds. Bake for 25–30 minutes until the top is golden, allowing it to cool to warm or room temperature to serve.

LEMON THYME AND LEEK TART

A sublime lunch or dinner that beautifully illustrates the power of the tweak. Make this with common thyme, lemon thyme or orange thyme and that slight shift in bias makes three very different tarts. Lemon thyme makes the sunniest, orange thyme is altogether more resinous and autumnal, and common thyme gives a tart you could eat for breakfast, lunch and tea and not tire of it.

You could make this with onion rather than leeks, and in a tart tin if you prefer. A swizz of herb oil or picada to serve is a fine option.

Serves 4–6

For the pastry

250g (9oz) plain (all purpose) flour, plus a little more for rolling

pinch of salt

150g (5oz) butter, cubed

1 medium egg, beaten

1 tsp picked lemon thyme leaves

For the filling

30g (1oz) butter

500g (1lb 2oz) leeks, white part only, thinly sliced

3 bay leaves

2 medium eggs

150g (5oz) sour cream or crème fraîche

1 tbsp picked lemon thyme leaves

¼ whole nutmeg, or to taste, grated

20g (¾oz) Parmesan or Cheddar, grated

sea salt and freshly ground black pepper

For the pastry, put the flour, salt and butter into a food processor and pulse until the mixture resembles fine breadcrumbs. Add the egg and pulse until the mixture just comes together. (Alternatively, mix the butter into the flour and salt in a bowl using your fingertips until it resembles breadcrumbs, then add the egg and mix to form a dough.) Bring the dough together with your hands, adding the thyme leaves, and shape into a round. Cling film (plastic wrap) the pastry and rest in the fridge for 30 minutes.

Melt the butter in a pan over a low-medium heat, add the leeks and bay leaves and cook for 15 minutes until really soft and sweet. Allow to cool a little.

Preheat the oven to 200°C/400°F/gas mark 6.

Beat the eggs in a bowl, then scoop out a couple of tablespoons of beaten egg to glaze later. Add the sour cream, thyme leaves and nutmeg to the bowl. Stir in the leeks and season to taste.

Remove the pastry from the fridge and roll out to a circle about 3mm (⅛in) thick, leaving no gaps or holes. Place a sheet of baking paper on a baking sheet, and put the circle of pastry on to it. Spoon the creamy leeks on top, spreading it out evenly and leaving a 1–2cm (½–¾in) gap around the edge. Fold the edge of the pastry over to create a lip. Nudge the bay leaves to the top. Glaze all exposed pastry with the reserved egg and sprinkle the cheese over the top of the filling.

Place the tart in the oven on a middle shelf and bake for 35–40 minutes until the pastry is crisp and pale golden and the tart filling is set. Remove from the oven and leave to cool for 5 or so minutes before cutting into wedges to serve.

DILL, LEMON AND GREEN BEAN PILAF

It's usually at about the sixth attempt that I finally stop my fork pecking at a plate of this. It is crazily moreish. By all means, make this with coriander, mint, lovage or chervil in any combination, but this is one of the places I love dill, and plenty of it. Whichever herb/s you choose, go big.

Serves 4–6

300g (10oz) basmati rice

400ml (14fl oz) chicken or vegetable stock

30g (1oz) butter

1 onion, thinly sliced

3 garlic cloves, finely chopped

2 bay leaves

big bunch of dill, stalks and leaves separated and both finely chopped

1 tsp ground cumin

1 tsp ground coriander

½ tsp ground turmeric

¼ tsp ground cinnamon

200g (7oz) green beans, stalk end trimmed (or use thin slices of courgette/zucchini)

finely grated zest of 1 unwaxed lemon

40g (1½oz) shelled pistachios (or use whole almonds), roughly chopped

sea salt and freshly ground black pepper

natural yoghurt and lemon wedges, to serve

Soak the rice in a bowl of cold water for 10 minutes, then drain well. Bring the stock to a bare simmer.

Melt the butter in a wide pan over a low-medium heat and cook the onion, garlic, bay leaves and dill stalks for 10 minutes until soft. Add the spices and ½ teaspoon salt and cook for a minute.

Add the rice to the pan, along with the beans and half of the dill leaves, stirring for 30 seconds to coat well and so it doesn't burn. Cover the rice with the hot stock, add the lemon zest and check the seasoning, adding salt and pepper to taste. Put the lid on and cook for 5 minutes over a high heat, then turn it down to the lowest heat and cook for 10 minutes until the stock is absorbed and the rice is just tender. Turn the heat off, remove the lid and place a tea towel over the pan, then return the lid and leave to rest for 5 minutes.

Fluff the rice with a fork, then scatter over the remaining dill and the nuts and serve immediately with yoghurt and lemon wedges on the side.

CURRY LEAF KEDGEREE

Most weekend mornings, I like a good breakfast. If it is leftover dinner squished on to toast with the back of a fork, I consider the day well started. As fine as this is on warm evenings or cold, I eat it happily anticipating breakfast the following day, having made too much for that very reason. This is really all about the curry leaves, but if you fancy parsley or coriander, go large, adding it on serving. Soft- or hard-boil the eggs as you like: for this, I simmer them for a minute, then leave in the water off the heat for another 6½ minutes for eggs with a mini yolk slide. Smoked mackerel works differently well, if you fancy a change from kippers.

Serves 4

300ml (10fl oz) milk

3 whole kippers

40g (1½oz) butter

1 large onion, finely chopped

20 fresh curry leaves (or use 10 dried)

3 garlic cloves, very finely chopped

250g (9oz) young spinach leaves (or use watercress)

2 tsp mild curry powder

½ tsp ground turmeric

300g (10oz) white basmati rice, rinsed and drained

300ml (10fl oz) vegetable or fish stock (or use water)

1 lemon, ½ for juice, the rest cut into wedges

4 soft-boiled eggs, peeled and quartered

sea salt and freshly ground black pepper

thinly sliced fresh green chilli, to serve (optional)

In a medium pan, bring the milk up to just below the boil. Cover the kippers with the milk and leave for 10 minutes. Strain, reserving the milk, then flake the kipper flesh, discarding the skin and any bones.

Melt 30g (1oz) of the butter in a pan and fry the onion and curry leaves for 10–15 minutes until soft. Meanwhile, cook the garlic and butter together in a separate pan for 30 seconds until aromatic, then add the spinach and stir until it has wilted. Set aside to drain.

Add the spices to the herby onion and cook for 30 seconds, then stir in the rice. Add the stock (or water) and 200ml (7fl oz) of the reserved milk and reduce the heat to low. Cover and cook without stirring for 15–20 minutes until the rice is tender and the liquid is absorbed. Stir through the spinach and fish, fluffing the rice as you go. Season with salt, pepper and the juice of half the lemon.

Serve in bowls topped with the egg quarters and sprinkled with the green chilli (if using). Serve the kedgeree with the lemon wedges.

FENNEL GRILLED RED MULLET WITH TOMATO AND FENNEL SALAD

Red mullet makes me smile. Firstly, it is such a fine fish, and secondly, it prompts me to remind an old friend that it was their haircut when we met. Fennel in vegetable or herb form reaches for the sky as it runs to seed, losing succulence in summer's heat, and while it retains its characteristic flavour, the texture toughens: this recipe is perfect for it. You could make this with sea bass, sardines or mackerel if you prefer.

Serves 4

12 cherry tomatoes, halved

2 fennel bulbs, thinly sliced

1 large shallot, thinly sliced

4 tbsp extra virgin olive oil

small bunch of flat-leaf parsley, leaves picked

juice of 1 lemon

4 red mullet, slashed a couple of times on each side

12 x 20cm (8in) stalks of fennel, with flowers if it's summer

sea salt and freshly ground black pepper

Preheat the oven to 190°C/375°F/gas mark 5.

Toss the tomatoes, sliced fennel and shallot in a roasting tin with 2 tablespoons of the olive oil and some salt and pepper. Bake for 15–20 minutes until soft, then stir through the parsley and half the lemon juice.

Use a fish cage if barbecuing (grilling), or a tin to grill (broil) in the oven. Preheat the grill to medium/high if using.

Rub a little olive oil into and over each fish and season with salt and pepper. Lay the fennel stalks on either side of the fish, pushing a few inside. Grill or barbecue for 4–6 minutes on each side, turning once or twice until the fish is just cooked through.

Serve the fish with the salad, and the driest, coldest white wine or a proper cider.

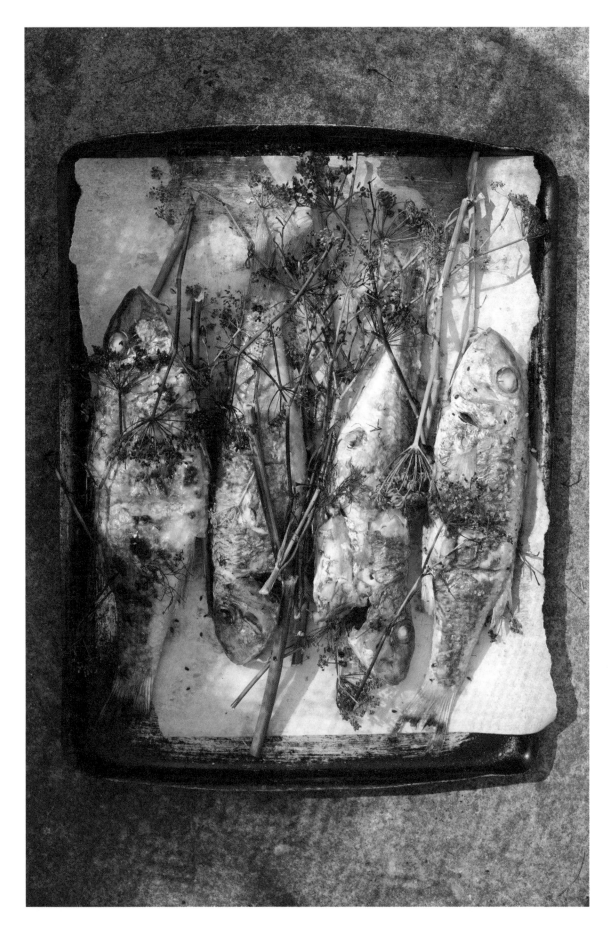

GRAVADLAX

I rarely eat salmon, but when I do it is very likely to be in this delicious form: cured in a sweet-salty mix, with or without the barest slick of peaty Islay whisky. The process is as old as the hills: the peppery, salty sugar cure draws moisture out of the raw flesh, passing its qualities into the flesh in exchange. This recipe's name comes from the time the fish would be buried in salt to preserve it; gravad means grave and lax is Swedish for salmon. As with many smoking and curing recipes, refrigeration means that the process is now more about imparting flavour than preservation.

A piece of salmon of fairly consistent thickness is ideal for an even cure; I usually go for two tail-end pieces and a 40-hour cure, but you can go for thick-end and up the timing to 48 hours. I like an Islay whisky in the cure; it brings a passing note of smoke to this.

With the cure scraped from the flesh it is ready to eat immediately, and dill mustard sauce (page 95) is the perfect accompaniment.

I also love gravadlax steamed: I got the idea from a Simon Hopkinson article. Set a pan of water with new potatoes over a high heat, reducing it to a bare simmer, place the fish in the steamer above it: 9 minutes with the lid on should do it. Remove the steamer and let it rest while the potatoes finish cooking. Slice as you would gravadlax (I prefer thicker than the norm: 6mm/¼in), leave the skin unserved, and accompany with the new potatoes covered in the dill mustard sauce.

Serves 6

1 tbsp black peppercorns, ground

60g (2¼oz) caster (superfine) sugar

60g (2¼oz) coarse sea salt

800g (1lb 12oz) side of salmon

2 tsp Islay whisky (optional)

80g (3oz) dill, roughly chopped

dill mustard sauce (page 95), to serve

Mix the ground peppercorns with the sugar and salt. Place the fish in a dish – I use a long plastic container – and slowly drip the whisky over the fish. Cover evenly with the salty sugar and scatter the dill on top.

Put a small board on top of the fish, place a few tins of beans or similar on top of the board to press down and accelerate the curing. Place in the fridge for 40 hours.

Use a knife to scrape the cure from the fish, slice thinly at an angle to the board and serve, skinless, with the dill mustard sauce.

GREEN CEVICHE

If the sun is shining and there's a cold bottle in the fridge, this is the lunch for you. The fish is cured in the lime juice – it doesn't need cooking – so prep time is minimal. If ever there was a recipe that shows off how to squeeze the abundant flavour from coriander stems, this is it. Vietnamese coriander makes a wonderful variation here, its lemon freshness setting off the lime beautifully.

This should be seriously fresh-tasting and lively in heat, taking you just through your place of comfort when you hope the heat might tail off, but not too far beyond.

Serves 4

300g (10oz) sustainable high-quality white fish, thinly sliced

juice of 2 limes

½ small onion, very finely chopped

1 jalapeño chilli, destemmed and roughly chopped (remove the seeds if you prefer less heat)

small bunch of coriander (cilantro), leaves and stems separated

1 small garlic clove, finely chopped

1 ripe avocado, finely chopped

½ cucumber, peeled, halved, deseeded and very finely chopped

sea salt and freshly ground black pepper

soft green lettuce leaves, to serve

Sprinkle the fish with ½ teaspoon salt and allow to sit for 20 minutes in the fridge, then squeeze over the juice of 1 lime.

Sprinkle the onion with a big pinch of salt and toss together. Leave for a few minutes, then rinse in cold water, drain well, squeeze over the juice of ½ lime and leave to one side.

Use a food processor or blender to blend the jalapeño chilli, coriander stems, 50ml (2fl oz) water, the remaining juice of ½ lime, garlic and a pinch of salt until it is a smooth purée.

In a mixing bowl, toss the fish with the purée, onion, avocado and cucumber. Season generously with salt and pepper and serve right away with the lettuce and coriander leaves.

MACKEREL WITH RAISINS, ORANGE AND PICADA

Picada is the star of this, forming a crisp herby crust that works with any fish but perhaps best with oilier favourites such as sardines and mackerel. It's usual to add picada late, but because the butterflied or filleted fish cook so quickly, the herbs aren't ruined in the oven.

This is so quick and delicious; honestly, have it for lunch on the next sunny day.

Serves 4

4 mackerel, butterflied or filleted

chilli flakes (optional)

4 tbsp olive oil

one batch of picada (page 109)

50g (2oz) raisins, plumped in warm water for 10 minutes, drained and patted dry

½ tsp fennel seeds, toasted and crushed

finely grated zest and juice of ½ small orange (or use lemon)

1 tbsp red wine vinegar

sea salt and freshly ground black pepper

Preheat the oven to 200°C/400°F/gas mark 6 and line a baking sheet with baking parchment.

Lay the fish fillets skin side up on the paper, season with salt and pepper and/ or the chilli flakes (if using) and drizzle with half the olive oil.

Mix together the picada, raisins, fennel seeds and orange zest. Flip the fish over so they are flesh side up and scatter the picada mixture over them. Bake in the oven until the fish is cooked, about 10 minutes. The topping should be crisp and golden. Meanwhile, whisk together the orange juice, vinegar and the rest of the olive oil. Remove from the oven and drizzle with the dressing before serving.

CRAB AND CHERVIL LINGUINE

I gave up booze for a few years when I started waking with the anticipation of what I might drink that day, by which token I should give up crab and chervil linguine, as if I eat it on a Monday it is exactly what I wake thinking of for the rest of the week.

Chervil and crab is a deeply pleasing combination: chervil's gentle parsley/aniseed flavour was made for the crab's sweet, salty breeziness. Tarragon, Korean mint, sweet cicely or parsley with fennel are excellent variations.

Serves 4

400g (14oz) linguine

1 tbsp olive oil

2 garlic cloves, finely chopped

good pinch of chilli flakes

2 tsp fennel seeds

finely grated zest of ½ unwaxed lemon

juice of 1 lemon

200g (7oz) brown crabmeat

200g (7oz) white crabmeat

small handful of chervil, finely chopped

sea salt and freshly ground black pepper

extra virgin olive oil, to finish

Cook the pasta in a large pan of salted boiling water until al dente.

Meanwhile, heat the olive oil in a frying pan over a medium-low heat and fry the garlic, chilli flakes and fennel seeds for a couple of minutes until soft but not coloured. Add the lemon zest and juice and then stir in the brown crabmeat.

Drain the pasta, reserving a few spoonfuls of the cooking water, and toss with the sauce, along with the white crabmeat and chervil. Add the extra water if the dish seems a little dry. Season to taste and divide between bowls.

Drizzle each bowl with a little extra virgin olive oil, and serve immediately.

FISH, LENTILS AND SALSA VERDE

There are certain creations at which I still marvel. I know manned space travel is an extraordinary thing but I'm still more mystified about how that box in the corner can pick up stations from around the world and relay events, music and news in real time. I feel similarly about salsa verde. Its inventor should be given the freedom of everywhere and everyone. I couldn't make up my mind whether to show it off at its best with puy lentils or a princely fish, so I went for both. The bream can be bass or firm, thick pieces of cod; the lentils are differently excellent if brown rather than puy. The fish can be grilled or barbecued, but I usually pan-fry it.

Serves 4

300g (10oz) puy lentils

2 bay leaves

3 tbsp olive oil

splash of red wine vinegar or lemon juice

4 fillets of sea bream

one batch of salsa verde, with perhaps a little left over (page 100)

sea salt and freshly ground black pepper

Rinse the lentils. Put them into a pan and cover with 1 litre (1¾ pints) cold water. Bring to the boil, skim off any froth that surfaces and add the bay leaves. Simmer for 20–30 minutes, adding salt 15 minutes into the cooking process, until the lentils are cooked through but still have some resistance. Drain and spoon into a bowl. Add about 1 tablespoon of the olive oil and a squeeze of red wine vinegar or lemon juice, and season to taste with salt and pepper. Cover to keep warm.

Add the remaining olive oil to a frying pan and place over a medium-high heat. Add the fillets, skin side down, and cook for 5 minutes or so – the skin should be lightly golden and crisping nicely but not crazily. Lower the heat to medium, flip each fillet over and cook until the flesh loses translucence – a couple of minutes. Share the lentils between each plate, place a fillet on each and adorn with salsa verde. Enjoy in the sun if there is any, but by the fire is equally good.

GRILLED PRAWNS WITH CHERMOULA

Prawns dashed with herbs, hot enough to make you regret not allowing them a minute to cool, are one of my favourite things. Even thinking of them snowbound in a blizzard of gremolata makes me salivate; smattered in a sandstorm of za'atar is equally good. Here with chermoula, the herbs come in two avalanches: half as a marinade, half dashed over the top once the prawns are cooked or served as a side. It shows how the same amalgamation of herbs – half cooked, half not – brings distinct layers of flavour. These are great on the barbecue, flesh side down.

Serves 4

16–20 large raw prawns (shrimp), shell on

one batch of chermoula (page 95)

Cut through the shell and flesh of the prawns lengthways with scissors or a sharp knife and arrange cut side up in a roasting tin. Spoon about 6 tablespoons of the chermoula over the flesh side and marinate for about 30 minutes.

Preheat the grill (broiler) to its highest setting. Place the tin under the grill and cook the prawns hard for 2–4 minutes, until bubbling and just cooked through and the shells are beginning to char. Serve with finger bowls and napkins (or just suck your fingers), and with the remaining chermoula to drizzle or dip as you like.

SCALLOPS IN A SEA OF HERBS

A small shop near the seafront where I live will rustle you up a quick fish bap, often filled with a dab or two, perfectly over-dusted with white pepper. It is a joy on a chilly sea wall with a wild wind taking the hair out of your eyes. Last time I went, I grabbed a dozen scallops without thinking of what might go with them. It turns out that what was in the fridge – a small bag of mangetout, the last few radishes, spring onions and two lemons, along with a couple of moments picking a few intense flavours from the garden – was all they needed. By all means choose a different range of herbs: whatever you fancy, whatever's to hand.

Serves 4

2 tbsp sunflower oil

12 scallops

200g (7oz) mangetout

4 spring onions (scallions), sliced on the angle

8 radishes, sliced

2 lemons, 1 juiced, 1 quartered

sea salt and freshly ground black pepper

A good half-handful each of:

green fennel leaves

coriander (cilantro) micros, or a few finely chopped coriander leaves

chive flowers, broken into florets

Korean mint leaves, finely chopped, plus a few flowers

Place a frying pan over a high heat and add 1 tablespoon of the oil. Season the scallops on one side. Once the pan is hot, place the scallops in the pan seasoned side down, following the numbers on a clock face, starting at 1 o'clock. Season the side facing upwards. Sear the scallops until caramelized, about 2–3 minutes. Use a spoon to turn them over in the order they were placed in the pan. Cook for a further 1–2 minutes, taking care not to overcook them. Do this in batches if you have a small pan. Remove the scallops to a plate and wipe the pan clean with kitchen paper.

Add the rest of the oil to the pan and, once hot, stir-fry the mangetout, spring onions and the radishes for about a minute. Stir through the lemon juice and the herbs and return the scallops to the pan to regain a little heat. Season with salt and pepper and serve with lemon quarters.

FISH STEW

This bold, bright delight sits somewhere between a broth, a soup and a stew; I've plumped for 'stew' purely as it feels a little more sustaining.

Here, bay and tarragon stalks build the base for the tarragon leaves to steal the show. Sweet cicely, fennel, or Korean mint are fine alternatives. Tarragon leaves darken with heat, so hold back a few to sprinkle on serving.

There are a few ways with this: if you have the fish bones you can create a deeply flavoured stock and later add just water, or use just stock, OR if you want it more intense, make it with bones *and* stock. The fish can be anything fairly meaty – a mix even – that looks good: bream, gurnard and sardines are superb.

Serves 4

4 tbsp olive oil

about 600g (1lb 5oz) fish bones, gills removed and cleaned of any blood (optional)

2 garlic cloves, finely chopped

1 fennel bulb, thinly sliced

2 celery sticks, thinly sliced

2 leeks, white parts only, thinly sliced

2 onions, thinly sliced

1 tsp fennel seeds

good pinch of chilli flakes, or more to taste

pinch of saffron (optional)

strip of orange peel (optional)

small bunch of tarragon, leaves and stalks separated

1 bay leaf

2 tbsp tomato purée (paste)

250ml (9fl oz) dry white wine

2 tomatoes, roughly chopped (or use whole tinned tomatoes)

1 litre (1¾ pints) fish stock or water (see above)

about 600g (1lb 5oz) fish fillets

sea salt and freshly ground black pepper

Heat the oil in a large pan over a medium heat and – if using – add the fish bones and cook for 5–10 minutes until lightly coloured. Reduce the heat a little, add the garlic and vegetables and cook for 15–20 minutes until soft, stirring frequently.

Stir in the spices, orange peel if using, tarragon stalks, bay leaf and tomato purée and cook for a few minutes, then add the wine and cook until reduced by half, stirring occasionally. Add the chopped tomatoes, stock or water and bring to the boil, then simmer for 10–15 minutes until the broth is slightly reduced. Strain, return to the pan and add salt and pepper to taste. Add the fish fillets and cook for a few minutes until the fish is just cooked through. Add the tarragon leaves to the pan and serve immediately with excellent bread.

LAKSA

The star of this spectacular soup is laksa leaf, aka Vietnamese coriander, with its creamy, bright, lemony coriander flavour. Mint and coriander in a 1:2 ratio works differently well. Don't be put off by the lengthy list of ingredients: it is as simple in creation as it is delicious.

Serves 4

3 tbsp sunflower

200ml (7fl oz) coconut milk

30g (1oz) tamarind paste

1 tsp shrimp paste (or use 1 tbsp fish sauce)

1 tbsp palm sugar (or use soft light brown sugar)

800ml (1½ pints) chicken stock or water

100g (3½oz) chicken, diced

pinch of salt

2 medium eggs, beaten

150g (5oz) dried rice vermicelli or 2 portions of pre-cooked noodles

150g (5oz) raw prawns (shrimp)

300g (10oz) beansprouts, or cucumber cut into matchsticks

1 bunch of spring onions (scallions), finely chopped

1 lime, ½ juiced and ½ cut into wedges

25g (1oz) bunch of Vietnamese coriander

sambal, chilli oil or sliced red chilli, to serve

For the paste

1 large shallot, chopped

3 garlic cloves, chopped

1 tbsp grated fresh ginger

1 lemongrass stalk, chopped

30g (1oz) roasted peanuts or cashews

½ tsp sea salt

2 tsp chilli flakes

2 tsp ground cumin

1½ tsp ground coriander

½ tsp ground star anise

¼ tsp ground cloves

¼ tsp grated nutmeg

¼ tsp ground cardamon

First make the paste. Blitz the shallot, garlic, ginger, lemongrass, nuts, 100ml (3½fl oz) water, salt and the spices in a food processor until smooth (add an extra splash of water if needed).

Heat 2 tablespoons of the oil in a large pan, add the paste and fry for 5–10 minutes, or until all the water has evaporated and the paste is starting to brown and stick to the bottom of the pan.

Stir the coconut milk, tamarind paste, shrimp paste or fish sauce, sugar and the stock into the paste, then bring to the boil. Add the chicken and simmer for 15–20 minutes until the chicken is cooked.

While the chicken is cooking, add the salt to the eggs and fry in the remaining oil in a small frying pan to form a thin omelette. Flip and cook on the other side, then remove from the pan and allow to cool. Roll up the omelette into a cigar shape and cut into thin strips.

Cook or soak the noodles as per the packet instructions, drain and divide between 4 bowls.

Add the prawns to the laksa and simmer for around 3 minutes until just cooked through. Add the beansprouts, spring onions and lime juice.

Top the noodles with the sliced omelette and a couple of ladles of laksa. Serve topped with roughly chopped coriander and a drizzle of the sambal or chilli oil, and lime wedges on the side.

GREEN CHICKEN CURRY

This green chicken curry is in the style of the Konkani coastal region of west India: full of green herbs and finished with yoghurt. If you like a Thai green curry, this is for you. Often as not, I make this with leftover roast chicken; I also up the spinach to three or four times this once in a while when the green urge calls. And fear not, coconut-dodgers, our nemesis sits very much in the background, drawing things together; I promise you will love this.

Serves 4

25g (1oz) desiccated coconut

1 tsp ground turmeric

75g (2½oz) yoghurt

500g (1lb 2oz) skinless and boneless chicken thighs, diced

3 tbsp vegetable or coconut oil

1 tbsp black mustard seeds

2 tsp cumin seeds

1 large onion, finely chopped

2 green chillies, finely chopped (deseeded for less heat), plus more to serve if you like

small bunch of mint, leaves only

small bunch of coriander (cilantro), roughly chopped

4 garlic cloves, finely chopped

1 tbsp grated fresh ginger

2 tsp garam masala

50g (2oz) spinach

2 tbsp cream (optional)

sea salt and freshly ground black pepper

Soak the coconut in 250ml (9fl oz) boiling water. Mix the turmeric, the yoghurt and ½ teaspoon salt together and stir through the diced chicken, then put to one side.

Heat the oil in a frying pan over a medium heat and cook the mustard and cumin seeds for 1–2 minutes until they begin to pop and sizzle. Add the onion and cook for 15 minutes, stirring occasionally, until soft.

Blend the coconut and its water with ½ teaspoon salt, the green chilli and the herbs (reserve a few leaves to serve) to a smooth sauce and put to one side.

Add the garlic and ginger to the onions and cook for 30 seconds until fragrant. Stir in the chicken and garam masala and cook for 5 minutes. Stir in the spinach and cook until wilted. Add the herb sauce and cook for 20–30 minutes until the chicken is cooked through and the sauce is rich and thick. Check the seasoning, adding salt and pepper to taste. Add the cream (if using) and cook for 1 minute. Top with the remaining herbs, chopped, and more sliced green chilli and serve with rice and/or flatbreads.

LAMB DHANSAK

Back in the day, a good friend returned from India with an uncharacteristic tan, a love of particular dishes and a digestive complaint of which we must never speak. Should we ever go out and have a little more than our daily ration, it was not unusual for us to have a late sit-down with a selection of curries, with him educating me as to their origins. Dhansak, traditionally a curry of mutton and lentils, ranked high on his favourites. I hope this version might one day find its way under his nose.

While the bay leaves are crucial to the sweet-spice base, it is the fenugreek leaf (aka methi) that steals all the glory at the end. While lamb/mutton is usual, this is excellent with chicken, prawns or mushrooms instead. Mint and coriander in place of the fenugreek leaf makes a very different, but very good variation.

Serves 4

600g (1lb 5oz) diced shoulder of lamb

50g (2oz) yoghurt

juice of ½ lemon

1½ tsp sea salt

1 tsp chilli powder, plus more to taste

3 tbsp ghee, butter or sunflower oil

2 onions, thinly sliced

5 cardamon pods, squashed a little

1 cinnamon stick

2 bay leaves

1 red chilli, finely chopped

5 garlic cloves, finely chopped

1 tbsp grated fresh ginger

2 tbsp garam masala

½ x 200g (7oz) tin chopped tomatoes

75g (2½oz) red lentils

30g (1oz) tamarind paste

1 tsp honey

2 tsp fenugreek leaf

Mix the lamb with the yoghurt, lemon juice, ½ teaspoon salt and 1 teaspoon chilli powder. Leave to one side.

Melt the ghee in a heavy-based pan over a medium heat, add the onions and whole spices and cook for 15 minutes or so until the onions are very soft and just beginning to colour. Add the fresh chilli, garlic and ginger and cook for 1 minute until softened, then add 1 teaspoon salt, more chilli powder to taste, and 1 tablespoon of the garam masala; cook for 1 minute until fragrant.

Add the lamb and cook for 10–15 minutes until the mixture just starts to stick to the pan. Add the chopped tomatoes, lentils and 700ml (1¼ pints) water, cover and cook for 45 minutes, stirring occasionally, until the lentils have completely broken down and the lamb is tender. Add the tamarind paste and the honey and cook for 5 minutes, adding a splash of hot water if required. Check salt, sweetness and acidity, adjusting to taste.

When ready to serve, sprinkle the curry with the remaining garam masala and the fenugreek leaf and serve with rice and/or naan bread.

GREEN SEASONING LAMB RUNDOWN

This is such a good curry and while fairly typically Jamaican, it has more than a touch of Trinidad about it, with the green seasoning marinade infecting the lamb with bright heat before cooking. The lamb fat slowly released as it cooks 'runs down' the meat and carries the herb and spice flavours into the vegetables. It really is quite something. Rundown is mostly about the thyme and the mix of vegetables, so do vary the meat – it is often made with fish – or just include more vegetables.

800g (1lb 12oz) diced lamb or goat

1 tsp ground turmeric

1–2 tsp Trinidad curry powder, or hot curry powder

one batch of green seasoning (page 99)

1 x 400ml (14fl oz) tin full-fat coconut milk

a mix of floury potatoes, sweet potatoes, unripe banana, squash etc., peeled and cut into large chunks, to make about 800g (1lb 12oz) prepared weight

200g (7oz) chard or robust spinach

1 lime, quartered

sea salt and freshly ground black pepper

In a large bowl, mix the meat with the turmeric, curry powder and green seasoning, cover and leave in the fridge overnight (or if time is against you, at least 2 hours).

Add the contents of the bowl to a large pan, add 100ml (3½fl oz) water and pour over the coconut milk. Bring to the boil, reduce the heat to a simmer, cover and cook for about an hour until just tender, adding a touch more water if it dries out, as you need enough volume to cook the potatoes later.

Season, adding salt, pepper or more curry powder to taste. Add the vegetable mix and the chard and cook for 20–30 minutes until tender and the liquid has largely cooked away. Add a squeeze of lime juice to taste.

MALAYSIAN FRIED CHICKEN IN CURRY LEAVES

The title of this recipe does all the water-carrying here; if you still need convincing after those six words, I can't help you. Cold beer is entirely appropriate.

Serves 4

600g (1lb 5oz) skinless and boneless chicken thighs, cut into bite-sized pieces

½ tsp ground turmeric

¼ tsp ground ginger

2 garlic cloves, finely chopped

1 ½ tbsp soy sauce

150g (5oz) self-raising flour

50g (2oz) cornflour (cornstarch)

2 tbsp curry powder

vegetable or sunflower oil, for frying

small bunch of curry leaves

1 red chilli, thinly sliced (optional)

sea salt and freshly ground black pepper

To serve

1 lime, cut into wedges

hot sauce

Mix the chicken with the turmeric, ground ginger, garlic, a generous amount of salt and pepper and the soy sauce. Mix the flour and cornflour with the curry powder and ½ teaspoon salt.

Get a separate bowl of water prepared and a baking sheet lined with baking parchment ready.

Dip the marinated chicken (in batches) into the flour mix, then briefly in the water, then quickly back into the flour, making sure it's well coated. Place on the baking sheet.

Carefully heat 3cm (1in) oil in a deep frying pan over a medium heat. It is ready for frying when a small cube of bread dropped into the oil sizzles immediately. Fry the chicken pieces, in batches, for 7–9 minutes until golden and crunchy and cooked through. Drain the chicken on kitchen paper.

Heat 2 tablespoons oil in a separate small frying pan and add the curry leaves and sliced chilli (if using). Add the chicken and gently fry for 2–3 minutes for the chicken to absorb the flavours. Serve with lime wedges and hot sauce – as hot as you can handle.

ZA'ATAR CHICKEN WITH THYME BUTTER
AND LAVENDER CELERIAC 'DAUPH'

A few minutes of setting up is all it takes for this three-pronged herbal attack to work its magic. While the za'atar-flavoured chicken skin is extraordinary – crisp, bright and sour with sumac and all the lemony Mexican oregano – the thyme butter is what drives this along, melting and basting the chicken breast, on its way to creating the buttery shallows in which the lavendered celeriac quietly surrenders. It is ridiculously good.

You can roast a three-dimensional chicken here, but spatchcocked is quicker and a butcher will do it for you, but don't hesitate to tackle it yourself: flip the bird over, breast side down, and use a pair of kitchen scissors to cut the spine out, then turn it over and use your hands against the breast to flatten the bird. There are so many variations around this theme: use a leg of lamb, add anchovies to the celeriac for a Jansson's temptation of sorts, perhaps make it with potato rather than celeriac, and you can always swap the thyme for rosemary, hyssop, English mace or oregano.

Don't overdo the water: it's a bit of a nerve-racker, trusting the butter to melt through the chicken in time to create a buttery bath in which the celeriac cooks, but it will.

Serves 4

1.2kg (2lb 10oz) celeriac, peeled

4 onions, thinly sliced

3 garlic cloves, finely chopped

2 long sprigs of rosemary

6 lavender flower heads, finely chopped

small bunch of thyme, leaves only

80g (3oz) butter

2kg (4½lb) chicken, spatchcocked

olive oil, for brushing

za'atar (page 110)

sea salt and freshly ground black pepper

Preheat the oven to 190°C/375°F/gas mark 5.

Cut the celeriac in half. Place cut side down on a chopping board and slice thinly; repeat with the second half. Spread half over the bottom of a large roasting tin and season well. Scatter the onions, garlic, rosemary and lavender over, and cover with the rest of the celeriac. Add just enough water to come a third of the way up the celeriac.

Use your fingers to work the thyme leaves into the butter until well incorporated. Carefully work the thyme butter under the skin and over the breast of the chicken, then press through the skin to distribute it fairly evenly. Place the chicken on top of the celeriac. Brush olive oil generously over the skin, then liberally dust with za'atar.

Place in the centre of the oven and cook for 1¼ hours or so, pressing down any celeriac in danger of colouring too much after 20 minutes. Check the chicken juices between the leg and body; if they don't run clear, allow another 10 minutes before checking with the other leg. Remove from the oven and allow to rest for 15 minutes before serving.

Serve with an excellent leafy salad or just-cooked mangetout, dressed with a sharp mustardy vinaigrette.

PORK AND GREEN SAUCE TACOS

These pork tacos are all growl and scowl, full of wonderful smoky chilli and deep intensity, until the green sauce fires a dash of bright refreshment across it, bringing it right back into line. The Mexican oregano sits deep within the sauce, yet rather than be lost when the embellishments are added, it seems more apparent after the green sauce hits the taco. You can substitute Mexican oregano with common oregano or avocado leaf, for a slightly different flavour – and by all means add a little mint to the green sauce if you fancy.

Serves 4

600g (1lb 5oz) diced pork belly or fatty pork shoulder

2 bay leaves

3 chipotle chillies, rinsed, destemmed and deseeded (or use chipotle in adobo)

1 large onion, finely chopped

2 tbsp sunflower oil

4 garlic cloves, finely chopped

1 tbsp ground cumin

1 tbsp paprika (smoked or unsmoked)

1 tsp ground allspice

1 tbsp Mexican oregano

2 tbsp red wine vinegar

1 tbsp honey or brown sugar

100g (3½oz) sour cream

4 tortillas

one batch of green sauce (page 98)

2 jalapeño chillies, thinly sliced

1 small red onion, very thinly sliced

½ bunch of coriander (cilantro), roughly chopped

sea salt and freshly ground black pepper

Place the pork in a heavy-based pan or casserole with the bay leaves, 300ml (10fl oz) water and 1 teaspoon salt. Cover and bring to the boil over a high heat, then reduce the heat to low and simmer for 45–60 minutes until most of the liquid has cooked away and the meat is tender, adding a splash of water if required.

While the meat is cooking, toast the chillies in a dry frying pan, then place in a bowl, cover with 200ml (7fl oz) boiling water and soak for 10 minutes.

Cook the onion in 1 tablespoon of the oil for 10–12 minutes until softened, then add the garlic, cumin, paprika, allspice and oregano and cook for a minute or so. Remove from the heat and stir in the vinegar and honey. Transfer to a blender along with the chillies and their soaking liquid and blend until smooth. Remove 2 tablespoons of the purée and put to one side to cool.

Stir the rest of the purée into the cooked pork and cook for about 15 minutes, or until the sauce is rich and thick. Check the seasoning, adding salt and pepper to taste.

Stir the cooled purée into the sour cream and season.

Build your taco, starting by filling a tortilla with the meat. Drench in green sauce and top with the chipotle sour cream, and slices of jalapeño and red onion. Finish off with the chopped coriander.

STEAK AND CHIMICHURRI

A few years ago an old friend and I took a couple of days out to walk a few dozen miles of our local coast. As the afternoon wore on and the lunchtime pints wore off, the wind blew so hard that we made laughing leaning towers into it, knowing that, were it to drop, noses might be dashed against the grass. The ground lifts, levels and drops like an ECG on that particular stretch, and as we descended towards the village to overnight, the relief was tempered only by the jab of blistered toes against the front of boots. On this final furlong, with the sun being lost to the sky behind us, the scent from the dusty, sandstone foot holes was as welcome as an old friend: oregano. I rubbed my hands over it, as if starting a fire with a stick; its oily green perfume taking me to places I've yet to visit. Later, deserved pints and steak, each mouthful against a backdrop of wild oregano as my fork rose to my mouth; ever since, that's how I want steak – with oregano – and when it comes with chimichurri's heat, so much the better.

I have only four opinions when it comes to steak: I salt and pepper it before cooking; I prefer thick to thin; resting is beyond essential; and how you like it (rather than how someone says it should be done) is best.

Serves 4

2 steaks, about 3–4cm (1 ¼–1 ½ in) thick

coarse or flaky salt and coarsely ground black pepper

one batch of chimichurri, with perhaps a little left over (page 102)

handful of chive flowers – garlic chive flowers if you have them

Take the steaks out of the fridge about 2 hours before cooking to come up to room temperature. Pat dry if they need it.

Heat a heavy cast-iron griddle or frying pan over a medium-high heat until very, very hot; better still, a cast-iron grill over a barbecue (grill).

Season the steaks generously (double what you might think) with salt and pepper and start cooking by pressing the fat edge (if the steak has one) on to the pan until browned.

Turn the steaks on to their side to sear, pressing down gently and turning every minute or so until both sides are deeply browned and they are done to your liking: a 3–4cm (1 ¼–1 ½ in) steak should take about 6 minutes for medium-rare. Allow the steaks to rest somewhere warm for 10 minutes before slicing to serve. Dash with chimichurri, serve extra in a pot, and shower with chive flowers.

MOLE VERDE

I grew epazote for the first time this year, and can highly recommend it to you if you dislike everything about yourself and take no joy from food. Picked fresh and at its perfect peak from the plant, it is a disgrace. You may as well suck your dog's bed. Dried, it is an entirely different entity – bitter, pungent and oddly refreshing, all in a good way. Here, with the Mexican oregano, it lays the scaffolding from which everything else is built.

Serves 4

1 onion, cut into wedges

200g (7oz) tomatillos (or use green or unripe tomatoes with a squeeze of lime)

2 fresh jalapeño chillies

2 poblano peppers, or use 2 green peppers and a couple of mild green chillies

4 garlic cloves, peeled

100g (3½oz) pumpkin seeds

100g (3½oz) spinach leaves

small bunch of coriander (cilantro), roughly chopped (reserve some to serve)

1 tsp dried epazote

1 tsp Mexican oregano (or use common oregano)

500ml (18fl oz) chicken stock (you may need less)

8 chicken thighs, skin removed if you prefer

4 tbsp olive oil or sunflower oil

sea salt and freshly ground black pepper

Heat a large frying pan and dry fry the onion, tomatillos, jalapeño chillies, peppers and garlic cloves for 10–15 minutes until lightly charred. Use a spoon to lift the charred vegetables into a bowl and cover to steam a little.

Toast the pumpkin seeds in the frying pan for 5 minutes until just beginning to pop, then put to one side.

Go through the vegetables, removing and discarding as much charred skin as possible, then tip the vegetables into a blender with the spinach leaves, coriander, pumpkin seeds (minus a few to serve), epazote and oregano. Blend to a smooth sauce, adding just enough stock to help.

Season the chicken with salt and pepper. In a good-sized frying pan over a moderate heat, add the oil and cook the chicken for 10 minutes until lightly coloured.

Add the herby sauce and cook for 15–25 minutes until the chicken is cooked through and the sauce is rich and thick, adding chicken stock as required. Season with salt and pepper to taste. Serve topped with the reserved pumpkin seeds and coriander.

PORCHETTA

I kept pigs until a few years ago, and even though I'd not eaten meat for many years previously, I felt surprisingly at home with that quiet exchange of their long, happy life foraging for roots and leaves, with a year's worth of delicious pork. I rarely eat pork now, but when I do I ensure it comes from animals who have led a pig's life. This is one of the best ways to roast pork, and although sage is the traditional herb for pork, I have to say I prefer rosemary. See if you do too. Serve this in rolls with apple and sage sauce and/or hot sauce, or with whatever vegetables (dauphinoise is so good here) you fancy.

Serves 8

1.5kg (3lb 5oz) piece of boneless pork belly, the skin scored in thin lines

400g (14oz) plain pork sausages, skins removed (or use mince or sausage meat)

8 garlic cloves, crushed

1 tbsp fennel seeds, toasted and crushed

2 large sprigs of rosemary, leaves stripped and finely chopped

200ml (7fl oz) white wine (or use stock or water)

sea salt and freshly ground black pepper

Place the pork belly skin side down on a clean surface, slash the flesh all over, about 1cm (½in) deep, and season with salt and pepper. Mix the sausage meat with the garlic, fennel seeds and rosemary, then smear the paste over the meat, pushing it into the slashes. Roll up tightly and tie up tightly with butcher's string at about 5cm (2in) intervals and place in the fridge, uncovered, for at least 1 hour, or overnight. Bring back to room temperature before cooking.

Preheat the oven to 160°C/325°F/gas mark 3.

Pat the outside of the pork belly dry and season generously with salt, then place on a rack in a roasting tin. Roast for 3–4 hours until the pork is easily pierced with a sharp knife. Remove from the oven and place the pork in a new tin lined with foil, then turn the oven up to full heat and roast for another 15–30 minutes, until the crackling is golden, making sure it doesn't scorch.

Remove from the oven and allow to rest in a warm place for at least 30 minutes. Meanwhile, remove the rack from the first tin and add the white wine (or stock or water), stir to loosen anything stuck to the roasting tin and pour the whole lot into a pan set over a medium heat. Boil until slightly thickened and season to taste.

Carve the pork into slices. Stuff into rolls and drizzle with sauce.

BEEF BRAISED IN ALE WITH PERSILLADE

If you are unsure of the value in layering herbs (and flavours in general) in your cooking, try this wonderfully autumnal braise. While you cook it, put on The Beatles' 'A Hard Day's Night': that first chord – a glorious, unnecessary CLANG before the verse kicks in – is a piece of heaven. The magic in this recipe and that clang belongs to the different layers that come together to create the whole. The bay and sage added early, half the persillade added late on, and the rest added to serve all build a glorious wave of flavour on the tongue. You could add all the herbs at once, as John, Paul and George might've played the same chord, but – as with George's 12-string F (with a G on the top and bottom and a C on the A string), D sus4 on John's 6-string, and Paul's genius D on the bass – it just isn't anything like the same.

A little liquid acidity just before serving draws the flavours more clearly into view: the excellent wares of Orkney Craft Vinegar and Cult Vinegar are great places to investigate.

Serves 4–6

1kg (2lb 4oz) ox cheeks – I cut them into 4–8 pieces, but cut into chunks if you prefer

1 tbsp olive oil

50g (2oz) butter

2 large onions, roughly chopped

2 celery sticks, roughly chopped

2 carrots, roughly chopped

200g (7oz) baby onions or small shallots, peeled and left whole

2 tbsp tomato purée, paste

6 garlic cloves, finely chopped

30g (1oz) plain (all purpose) flour

330ml (11fl oz) ale

300ml (10fl oz) stock, beef ideally (or use chicken or vegetable)

2 bay leaves

1 tbsp finely chopped sage

8 tbsp persillade (page 112)

splash of excellent vinegar, or lemon juice

sea salt and freshly ground black pepper

Preheat the oven to 150°C/300°F/gas mark 2.

Season the beef with salt and pepper. Warm the oil in a large casserole over a high heat and cook the beef until brown all over. Remove from the pan with a slotted spoon and set aside.

Add the butter and the vegetables and cook for 10 minutes over a medium heat until the vegetables soften. Add the tomato purée and garlic and cook for 5 minutes more. Then add the flour and stir well to combine. Add the ale, whisking continuously to prevent lumps, then the stock, continuing to whisk. Return the beef to the casserole along with the bay and sage and increase the heat to high. Bring to a boil, then reduce to a gentle simmer.

Cover the casserole and transfer to the oven. Braise for 2½–3 hours, until the meat is extremely tender, adding 4 tablespoons of the persillade after 2 hours. Add a little water or stock if the tideline drops below halfway on the islands of meat.

When cooked, remove from the heat and allow to rest for 10 minutes. Season to taste with salt and pepper, then stir in a tablespoon of vinegar or lemon juice: taste and add a little more if you fancy. Serve with mash or crushed potatoes, topping with the remaining persillade.

SWEET THINGS

FIG LEAF AND LEMON VERBENA RICE PUDDING

As with blackcurrants, figs are a fruit given a serious run for their money in the kitchen by their aromatic leaves. Infused here, their Shredded Wheat maltiness takes care of the lower end of the flavour spectrum and lemon verbena the high. If you have a cardamom plant, try three fresh leaves instead of the fig leaves.

Serves 4

650ml (22fl oz) whole milk

3 dried fig leaves (page 119)

2 pared strips of orange zest

120g (4oz) arborio rice, washed

15 lemon verbena leaves

40g (1½oz) caster (superfine) sugar

20g (¾oz) butter

10g (⅓oz) demerara sugar

seeds from 3 cardamom pods, ground

Pour the milk into a pan, add the fig leaves and orange zest and bring to a simmer. Add the rice, stir, and bring back up to the boil and then down to a gentle simmer. Cook, stirring often, picking out the now-limp fig leaves after 10 minutes and adding the lemon verbena. It should take 25–35 minutes for the rice to cook.

Stir in the caster sugar, add the butter and add a touch more milk if needed.

Preheat the grill to high. Pour the creamy rice into an ovenproof dish, sprinkle with demerera and the ground cardamom, and flash under the grill until a just-browning skin forms.

THYME AND PARSLEY HONEY BREAD AND BUTTER PUDDING

As a very young kid, I remember being aghast when the old man said his favourite (and long not eaten) dessert was bread and butter pudding; it sounded like something from the war, and clearly inferior to my beloved butterscotch Instant Whip. He would have liked this. As with lamb chops, if I eat bread and butter pudding all I want to eat for the next three days is bread and butter pudding. Common thyme is great in this, but lemon thyme adds a fresh zing that I prefer in the warmer days, and orange thyme for the colder.

Parsley honey (page 116) is perfect here, though apricot jam makes a fine substitute.

Serves 4–6

150g (5oz) butter, softened

300g (10oz) brioche loaf, cut into thick slices

90g (3¼oz) parsley honey (page 116) or apricot jam

4 bay leaves

3 medium eggs

60g (2¼oz) demerera sugar, plus more to sprinkle

3 tbsp Islay whisky (or brandy)

300ml (10fl oz) whole milk

2 tsp orange thyme (or use lemon or common thyme), leaves picked

50ml (2fl oz) double (heavy) cream

Butter each slice of brioche, then sandwich 2 slices together with a good dollop of the parsley honey (or jam). Cut each in half into triangles and arrange in a baking dish snugly, pushing the bay leaves into a few gaps, and smearing any remaining butter over the top.

Whisk the eggs and sugar together, then whisk in the whisky (or brandy), milk, thyme and cream. Pour the custard over the brioche sandwiches, pushing the bread down into the liquid so that it is completely covered. Leave to soak for 30 minutes.

Preheat the oven to 180°C/350°F/gas mark 4.

Brush with the remaining parsley honey or jam and sprinkle with demerara sugar. Bake for 35–40 minutes until golden and risen. Leave to cool for 10 minutes before diving in with spoons. To my shame, I like this with unnecessary double cream.

LEMON LAVENDER MERINGUES

Lavender is a cheery little sod, but can all too easily be a bit much in cooking. Don't let that put you off though; if you get it right, that half-scent-half-flavour makes it a delightful transformer. The amount to add here depends on how you intend to enjoy the meringues: five flower heads is perfect for something simple, but if you are using the meringues in a tumbled coming together of other ingredients – such as the Eton mess on page 234 – you can afford to up it to 8 to retain impact.

A kitchen mixer makes this easiest; otherwise have someone else tip the sugar in while you whisk. I like these meringues so that they are crisp but softer-centred, part tearing, part breaking in half when you try to split them.

Makes about 10

300g (10oz) caster (superfine) sugar

5–8 lavender flower heads (see above), broken up

slice of lemon

5 medium egg whites

finely grated zest of 1 unwaxed lemon

Preheat the oven to 130°C/250°F/gas mark 1.

Whizz 40g (1½oz) of the sugar with the lavender flower heads in a coffee/ spice grinder to create lavender sugar. Stir this thoroughly through the rest of the sugar.

Line a baking sheet with baking parchment and spread the sugar across it. Place it in the oven and warm it for 6–8 minutes.

Wipe the side of a large bowl (or the bowl of a stand mixer) with the lemon slice to ensure it is entirely grease-free. Add the egg whites and lemon zest to the bowl and whisk on high, adding the warmed sugar gradually. Whisk until the meringue becomes glossy and holds its shape in soft peaks. Spoon the meringue in 10cm (4in) dollops on the baking sheet, a few centimetres apart.

Place in the oven for a couple of hours. When they are crisp on the outside and lift off the parchment easily, take them out of the oven. Let them cool completely and store in an airtight container if not using immediately.

LAVENDER, STRAWBERRY AND RHUBARB ETON MESS

Eton mess is trifle for the lazy, a tumble of in-season fruit, half buried in an avalanche of meringue and cream, and stirred through just enough that you might find a hidden 50p. It is pretty hard to get wrong, just don't make it too sweet. A little sourness is crucial – here supplied by the rhubarb. I often make this with gooseberry curd, elderflower cordial as the syrup, passion fruit pulp or whatever might be at its peak.

I originally wrote this as a single recipe, but loved two of its constituent parts – the lemon lavender meringues and the cooked rhubarb – so much that I wanted to be sure you could enjoy them separately, as they are so good.

Serves 4–6

400ml (14fl oz) double (heavy) cream

240g (8½oz) strawberries, halved or quartered depending on size

4 lemon lavender meringues (page 232)

270g (9½oz) rose and lemon verbena rhubarb (page 249)

Whip the cream until it holds a floppy quiff.

Put the strawberries into a large bowl. Break the meringues into pieces and fold them into the cream; stir this into the strawberries until semi-incorporated. Add the rhubarb – only slightly combining – and spoon over the syrup that comes with it. Serve with a big spoon and see how much people come back for.

PISTACHIO, LEMON VERBENA AND ROSE SCENTED GERANIUM ICE CREAM

This is a wonderful coming together of flavours, where the balance can very easily tip towards the rose in early summer when the oils are high and the flavour and scent fullest, or more towards the lemon verbena later in the year; either way, it is extraordinary. The saffron may not be the star here, but it quietly anchors the whole from being too sweet or dominated by a single flavour. If you don't like the idea of pieces of pistachio, feel free to swizz the lot to a fine texture, but remember I am judging you.

Makes about 900ml (1½ pints)

120g (4oz) unsalted, shelled pistachios

400ml (14fl oz) whole milk

300ml (10fl oz) double (heavy) cream

good handful of rose scented geranium leaves

12 or so lemon verbena leaves

good pinch of saffron

5 medium egg yolks

150g (5oz) caster (superfine) sugar

Dry fry the pistachios in a large, dry frying pan over a medium heat until the merest hint of darkening here and there. Leave to cool a little, then whizz half in a food processor until fine. Chop the rest by hand into coarse pieces.

Warm the milk and cream together in a medium-sized pan over a medium heat, stirring occasionally until it just comes to the boil. Reduce to a simmer. Add the geranium leaves, lemon verbena leaves and saffron and keep just at a bare simmer for 10 minutes.

Beat the yolks and sugar together until pale and smooth, then stir in the finely whizzed pistachios.

Pour the scented creamy milk through a sieve into a large jug. Stirring constantly, pour into the egg mixture and, once thoroughly combined, return to the pan. Heat gently, whisking frequently, until it forms a slightly thicker custard – it won't go as far as custard usually goes, just thicker than it started. Cover and allow to cool.

Churn in an ice cream maker if you have one, stirring through the remaining pistachios just before it freezes fully. Alternatively, pour into a plastic tub and freeze for a few hours before spooning into a blender and whizzing briefly, pouring back into the tub, adding the pistachios, and returning to the freezer.

TARRAGON AND OLIVE OIL ICE CREAM

What an elegant ice cream this is, full of tarragon's gentle aniseed and the silk of olive oil. Use very fresh tarragon to get the fullness of its flavour, and a good fruity (rather than peppery) oil. Depending on what you eat before you serve this, you may feel this needs a little straightening out with flaky salt, pomegranate molasses, extra oil or even a few chilli flakes over the top. A shot of gin can soften the texture and the sweetness if you fancy. Thai basil, Korean mint and sweet cicely make fine alternatives to tarragon.

Makes 900ml (1½ pints)

250ml (9fl oz) double (heavy) cream

300ml (10fl oz) whole milk

bunch of tarragon, leaves stripped from half

6 large egg yolks

140g (4½oz) caster (superfine) sugar

120ml (4fl oz) extra virgin olive oil

good pinch of salt

Pour the cream and milk into a medium pan with the half bunch of tarragon that isn't stripped and bring gently to a simmer.

Meanwhile, put the egg yolks, sugar and tarragon leaves into a blender and blitz on low speed, increasing to high briefly. Add the oil and salt and blend again, increasing the power until a smooth consistency forms.

Pour the hot creamy milk through a sieve into a jug. Turn the blender on low, and pour the creamy milk very slowly into the oily tarragon mixture. When fully incorporated, pour the mixture back into the pan and heat gently, whisking frequently, until it thickens a little. Cover and allow to cool.

Churn in an ice cream maker if you have one, or pour into a plastic tub and freeze for a few hours before spooning into a blender and whizzing briefly, pouring back into the tub and returning to the freezer. Remove from the freezer 20 minutes prior to serving to make it easier to scoop.

THREE LEMON SORBET

This is fresher than Mae West after three gins. While you can do without one of the sources of lemon, they each sing the same note differently and it is this chorus I like best. Something like a pinot grigio is good here; dry, but not the full camel's flipflop. The result is sharp, bright, with just the right amount of sweetness, and just slightly on the slushy side.

Makes 1 litre (1¾ pints)

2 lemongrass stalks

350g (12oz) caster (superfine) sugar

600ml (1 pint) water

pared zest and juice of 2 unwaxed lemons

50 lemon verbena leaves

200ml (7fl oz) dry white wine

Lightly bash the lemongrass stalks with a rolling pin so that they resemble a Bic pen you've trodden on. Dissolve the sugar in the water in a large pan over a medium heat, stirring occasionally, then add the lemongrass and bring just to the boil. Remove from the heat and add the strips of lemon zest and the lemon verbena leaves.

Allow to completely cool. Strain the herbs and zest out, and then add lemon juice and wine.

If you have an ice cream maker, use it in the usual way. If not, pour into a plastic tub and freeze. After around 4 hours, when the sorbet is half frozen, whisk or whizz in a blender until smooth and return to the freezer. Repeat if you have the patience of a saint.

Remove the sorbet from the freezer about 15 minutes before serving, to make it easier to scoop.

RHUBARB AND BLACKCURRANT LEAF
GIN AND TONIC SORBET

Blackcurrant leaf sorbet has long been among my very favourite sorbets, but this combination pips it. Fresh, cheeringly optimistic and welcome at the end of a meal of just about anything.

Makes 1 litre (1¾ pints)

200g (7oz) caster (superfine) sugar

300ml (10fl oz) water

400g (14oz) rhubarb, cut into 5cm (2in) pieces

2 large handfuls of young blackcurrant leaves

juice of 2 lemons

4 tbsp gin

150ml (5fl oz) tonic water

Dissolve the sugar in the water in a large pan over a medium heat, stirring occasionally, until just coming to the boil. Reduce to a bare simmer and add the rhubarb. Poach for 10 minutes, remove from the heat and then add the blackcurrant leaves.

Allow to completely cool. Pick out and discard the leaves. Stir in the lemon juice, gin and tonic.

Pour the fruity syrup into a blender and whizz until completely smooth. If you have an ice cream maker, use it in the usual way. If not, pour into a plastic tub and freeze. After around 4 hours, when the sorbet is half frozen, whisk or blend until smooth and return to the freezer. Repeat after a couple of hours, if you remember.

Remove the sorbet from the freezer about 15 minutes before serving, to make it easier to scoop.

BAY CHESTNUT CHOCOLATE CHERRY CAKE

As wonderful as bay smells, if you suck on a leaf you'll be assailed by waves of bitter unexpecteds. Sugar syrups, milk infusions, water, stock and oil leave that bitterness unmined, while providing a taxi for its best qualities straight to your taste buds.

This cake – pretty much a torte – is marvellous without the bay, but the leaves bring warmth and comfort, and add complexity of flavour like that friend who embellishes a group conversation without making it about them. The bay's flavour is stronger when the cake has had some time in the fridge, or next day. The leaves on the top are there for you to peel off and scrape – as you might the flesh from an artichoke petal – the beautifully infused cake that clings to it.

You can make this with 180g (6oz) butter instead of the oil if you prefer; I just happen to love chocolate and olive oil cakes, and they tend to keep longer, though that's rarely an issue. Because I'm your pal, I've made this to suit the typical packet-size of ready-cooked chestnuts and chocolate.

Serves 6–8

180ml (6fl oz) whole milk

180g (6oz) cooked chestnuts

18 bay leaves

200g (7oz) dark (bittersweet) chocolate, broken into smallish pieces

4 medium eggs, separated

110g (4oz) caster (superfine) sugar

140ml (5fl oz) olive oil

12 cherries, stoned and torn almost in half

Preheat the oven to 180°C/350°F/gas mark 4. Line the base and sides of a 20cm (8in) round cake tin with baking parchment.

Put the milk, chestnuts and 12 of the bay leaves into a pan and slowly bring to a simmer.

Spoon the bay leaves out of the milk and discard them. Add the chocolate pieces, stirring frequently until melted and a smooth sauce forms. Briefly whizz in a blender – leaving a little texture here is good.

Stir or whisk the egg yolks and sugar together in a large bowl until fully combined. Add the oil a little at a time, whisking to combine. Whisk in the chestnutty milk.

Whisk the egg whites into soft peaks – a peak should hold a quiff at its tip. Using a large spoon, add a spoonful of egg white to the chocolatey mix to loosen it, then fold the rest in. Pour into the cake tin, using a spatula to scrape out as much as possible. Dot with the cherries, then place 5–6 bay leaves on the surface. Bake for 30 minutes or so: it should have the merest wobble to the centre.

Cool for 5 minutes then turn on to a cooling rack.

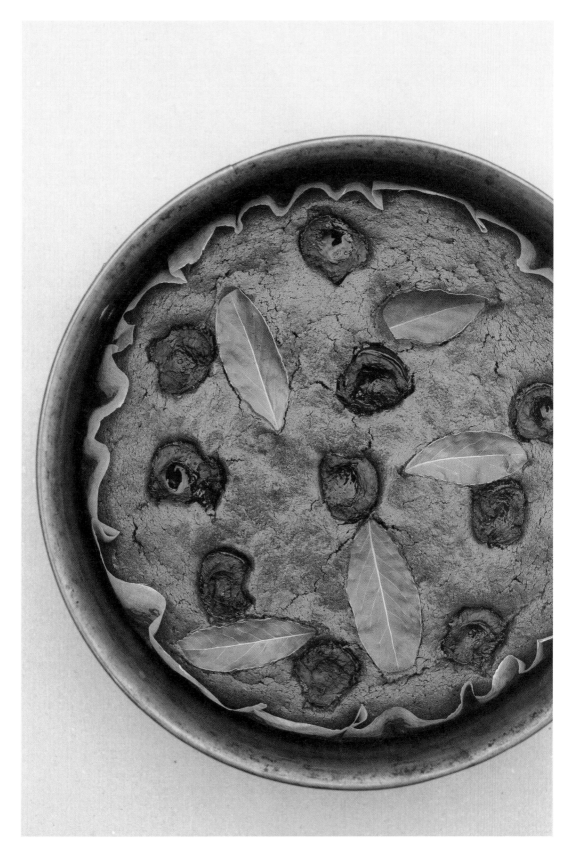

PINEAPPLE AND SAGE UPSIDE DOWN CAKE

Ever since the sweet and sour apricot upside down cake in my last book *Sour*, my love for a topsy-turvy treat has been rekindled. This latest incarnation pairs the sweet/sour brilliance of pineapple with the piney, deep green resinousness of sage, and a very special alliance they form. Ginger rosemary is so good in place of the sage too. A little sage syrup poured over may suit those with a sweeter tooth.

Serves 6–8

50g (2oz) butter, plus more for greasing

15 sage leaves

150g (5oz) caster (superfine) sugar

100g (3½oz) soft light brown sugar

150g (5oz) plain (all purpose) flour

1 tsp ground cardamom (or star anise)

1 tsp bicarbonate of soda (baking soda)

½ tsp salt

1 small pineapple, peeled, cored and cut into chunks

4 eggs

100ml (3½fl oz) sunflower oil

Preheat the oven to 180°C/350°F/gas mark 4. Lightly butter and line a 25cm (10in) cake tin with baking parchment.

Swizz half of the sage leaves with the caster sugar in a blender to make sage sugar.

Melt the butter and the brown sugar together in a pan over a medium heat, stirring to combine. Add the remaining sage leaves and allow to infuse off the heat for a few minutes.

Sift the flour, cardamon, bicarbonate of soda and salt into a bowl and mix in the sage sugar; put to one side.

Pour the sugary sage butter into the cake tin and place the pineapple pieces on top.

Whisk the eggs and oil together, then combine into the dry ingredients. Pour the batter into the cake tin, place in the centre of the oven and bake for 40 minutes or so until a skewer comes out clean.

Cool on a wire rack for 5 minutes, then place a plate on top and carefully turn the cake upside down and out on to the plate. Serve warm or at room temperature, with whichever cream or yoghurt takes your fancy.

LEMON VERBENA AND RASPBERRY CAKE

Since the cardboard tray was removed from the Bounty Bar (and as John Shuttleworth rightly pointed out, caused a mutiny over the Bounty) I have protested in the strongest terms, i.e. not eating the occasional bar as I used to. Other than that bar, I rarely enthuse about coconut, but this cake is an exception. As well as adding its characteristic flavour and texture, the soft filaments of desiccated coconut seem to hold so much of the flavour of the lemon verbena syrup poured over this beautifully scented cake.

The double impact of both herb sugar and herb syrup is so very pleasurable here.

This is a hugely adaptable cake: use lemongrass or pineapple sage for the sugar and syrup, and it's a great recipe to make as a loaf in a 900g (2lb) tin or double in size for a 24cm (9½in) cake tin. And if you are a coconut refuser, use almond flour instead.

Serves 6–8

120g (4oz) caster (superfine) sugar, plus 3 tbsp for the syrup

10 lemon verbena leaves, finely chopped

160g (5½oz) butter

2 medium eggs, lightly beaten

100g (3½oz) plain (all purpose) flour

1 tsp baking powder

80g (3oz) desiccated coconut

2 tbsp milk

80g (3oz) raspberries

juice of 1 lemon (or 2 limes)

Preheat the oven to 180°C/350°F/gas mark 4. Lightly butter a 20cm (8in) cake tin and line it with baking parchment.

In a spice grinder or small food processor, blitz the 120g (4oz) sugar and 5 of the lemon verbena leaves thoroughly. Transfer to a large bowl.

Add the butter, and beat on high for about 5 minutes until pale and creamy. While still beating, add half the egg to the butter and sugar a little at a time. Add a tablespoon of the flour to help prevent the mixture from curdling, then continue adding the egg.

Sift the flour and baking powder and add this to the cake mix, beating briefly with a large spoon to combine. Add the coconut and the milk – the mixture should be loose enough to drop off the back of a spoon; if not, add more milk just a little at a time until it does.

Spoon half the mix into the prepared tin and scatter with the raspberries, then spoon over the remaining cake mix. Bake in the oven for 45–50 minutes until a skewer inserted into the middle of the cake comes out clean.

While the cake bakes, make the syrup. Put the lemon or lime juice, 2 tablespoons of water and the 3 tablespoons caster sugar into a small pan and boil rapidly for 2 minutes or so until the liquid becomes syrupy. Add the remaining lemon verbena leaves and leave to infuse until the cake is cooked, then strain.

Remove the cake from the oven and drizzle with the syrup while warm. Serve when cooled at least a little – yoghurt or crème fraîche is good to go with.

QUADRUPLE FIG, LEMON VERBENA AND SHERRY TRIFLE

My oldest friend says little of consequence, which is one of the reasons I love him dearly. Once in a while, like a monkey with a typewriter, a golden sentence is formed, never better than when he rang to tell me: 'The best way to eat trifle is with The Big Spoon, dressed only in your pants, bathed in the light from the fridge.' Amen to that.

This won't be the cheapest trifle you'll ever make but it really is worth the occasional splash out. It has figs in four forms: fresh, dried, fig leaf syrup and fig leaf custard. It is all set off by a very present sherry, the lemon verbena, a dusting of herb sugar and a rubble of pistachios.

You can use a calmer sherry but PX has its showing-off shirt and dancing boots on, and that's exactly what I love here. The custard, syrup and herb sugar can all be substituted as you fancy: bay custard, sage or lemon verbena syrup (or even pomegranate molasses) and basil sugar or something sharp like passion fruit dust (see suppliers on page 266) would be superb. Madeira cakes vary so much that to provide a weight is pointless; use a piece about the size of your mobile and 5cm (2in) thick. You can make the cake if you fancy but it is really just a granular vehicle for the sherry; sponge fingers would be great too. Make this as a big sharing bowlful, or as individuals.

Serves 4

200ml (7fl oz) sherry – something intense like Pedro Ximénez

30g (1oz) caster (superfine) sugar

1 generous sprig of lemon verbena

12 large figs, quartered

For the custard

300ml (10fl oz) whole milk

300ml (10fl oz) double (heavy) cream

5 dried fig leaves (page 119)

5 medium egg yolks

70g (2½oz) caster (superfine) sugar

2 tbsp cornflour (cornstarch), blended with 2 tbsp water until smooth

Place the sherry in a pan with the sugar and lemon verbena and warm over a medium heat to a bare simmer. Lower the fig quarters into the liquid and poach until soft but not collapsing. Remove from the heat and allow to cool.

Warm the milk, cream and fig leaves in a medium heavy-based pan and bring it slowly to the boil. Remove from the heat and allow to infuse as the mix cools a little.

Whisk the egg yolks and sugar in a bowl until pale and thick. Remove the fig leaves from the warm creamy milk. Slowly add the warm mixture to the bowl, stirring it constantly into the sugary egg yolks until well combined. Tip the mixture back into the pan, using a rubber spatula to scrape as much as possible, and warm over a low-medium heat.

Cook for 10 minutes or so, stirring constantly. You'll feel the custard start to thicken; reduce the heat a touch if this is happening too quickly for comfort. The custard will thicken enough to coat the back of a wooden spoon, at which point turn off the heat.

Continued overleaf

To assemble and finish

50g (2oz) pistachios, roughly chopped

Madeira sponge cake, roughly chopped

300ml (10fl oz) double (heavy) cream

100g (3½oz) crème fraîche

140g (4½oz) mascarpone

4 dried figs, thinly sliced

generous drizzling of fig leaf syrup (page 119)

generous dusting of Korean mint sugar (page 106)

Use your fingers to blend the cornflour mixture if it has separated a little, then stir it into the custard. Place back on the heat for a couple of minutes, stirring constantly to prevent sticking and to keep it smooth: the custard will become very thick. Remove it from the heat. Place a damp tea towel over the top of the pan to prevent the custard forming a skin as it cools.

Toast the crushed pistachios briefly over a medium-high heat in a dry pan. A little light darkening and intensifying of colour is what you are looking for, rather than scorch.

To assemble the trifle: crumble the Madeira cake into the bottom of a serving bowl (or individual bowls) and drown it with sherried figs. Pour the custard over the top and refrigerate until set.

Whisk the double cream, crème fraîche and mascarpone in a large bowl until thick and combined, and use a spatula to gently spoon and spread it across the custard. Scatter the cream with pistachios and dried fig slices, drizzle plentifully with the syrup and dust generously with herb sugar.

Put the trifle in the fridge, pop the heating on and return only in your pants, while everyone sleeps, Big Spoon in hand.

ROSE AND LEMON VERBENA RHUBARB

This is delicious, easy and quick to prepare: the slow cooking draws out the flavours to create a little intense syrup that goes really well with the main season's sharp rhubarb. This won't be wildly sweet, which makes it perfect as part of the Eton Mess on page 234, and this is how much to make for that dessert. By all means add honey to serve with yoghurt if your sweet tooth tugs at your hem.

From time to time I'll cook this on the hob with a little more liquid, which gives a slightly softer result to the rhubarb.

Serves 4

15 rose scented geranium leaves

15 lemon verbena leaves

30g (1oz) caster (superfine) sugar

5 good stalks of rhubarb, around 400g (14oz), cut into 2cm (¾in) pieces

Preheat the oven to 130°C/250°F/gas mark 1.

Scatter the leaves in the bottom of an oven dish, shower in the sugar and place the rhubarb on top. Pour in just enough water to form a lake under the rhubarb. Roast, uncovered, for about 40 minutes, flipping the rhubarb after 15 minutes if you remember, until the rhubarb is soft but retains its shape.

ROSE SCENTED GERANIUM BAKLAVA

I have no 'off' button with baklava; if it is in the house, it whispers my name at a frequency that – like a dog whistle – is heard only by the creature intended, so I make it only once or twice a year to avoid looking like a balloon full of yoghurt.

An intense syrup is the key to this, so taste it with more attention than you usually might before extracting the leaves. Star anise and rose talk to each other so well in this, but it works wonderfully with lemon verbena leaves too.

The recipe calls for what is usually slightly too much butter (200g/7oz is probably enough) but you want no sense of being short of it in the run-in to buttering the top layers.

Makes more than you need and less than you want

400g (14oz) walnuts

8 cardamom pods, seeds only

½ sheriff's badge of star anise

1 tsp fennel seeds

4 tbsp granulated sugar

12 sheets of filo pastry

230g (8oz) unsalted butter, melted

For the syrup

100g (3½oz) dark muscovado sugar

300g (10oz) caster (superfine) sugar

30 rose scented geranium leaves

1 tbsp lemon juice

Preheat the oven to 180°C/350°F/gas mark 4.

Reduce the walnuts to a coarse rubble using a tea towel and rolling pin (there's always someone to think about here) or in the food processor. Take 30g (1oz) of the walnut rubble and bash to reduce it further; set aside.

Whizz the cardamom, star anise and fennel seeds together with the sugar in a coffee/spice grinder or a mortar and pestle. Mix with the larger walnut rubble.

Place a sheet of greaseproof paper in an 18 x 28cm (7 x 11in) baking tin. Lay a sheet of filo pastry in the tin (it will probably overlap the edges) and brush with melted butter. Place a second sheet on top of the first, brush with butter and repeat until you have 6 layers of filo.

Spoon the nut mixture over the pastry. Repeat the filo/butter layering with six sheets, as before. Use a very sharp knife to cut just the top six layers of pastry into 5 x 3cm (2 x 1in) rectangles, and then diagonally in one direction so each rectangle is cut into two triangles.

Bake for 20 minutes in the centre of the oven, then lower the temperature to 150°C/300°F/gas mark 2 and cook for another 25 minutes until golden.

While the baklava is cooking, make the syrup. Warm the sugars and 250ml (9fl oz) water over a medium heat, stirring occasionally to encourage the sugar to dissolve. Simmer for a few minutes, then remove from the heat. Add the scented geranium leaves and lemon juice and allow to infuse for 5 minutes or so. Pour into a jug, using a sieve to catch the leaves.

Once the baklava has cooled for 5 minutes out of the oven, pour the syrup over, then sprinkle with the finely crushed walnuts and leave to cool further.

Follow the grid of cuts to slice the baklava. Then make an excellent coffee and try not to eat it all at once.

HERB SHORTBREAD

I do love a biscuit. And especially one with a recipe of such memorable quantities. As a mid-morning mood shifter or a sidecar to a sorbet's motorbike this shortbread is hard to beat.

This mixture is shorter than Danny DeVito's miniskirt – this gives a wonderful texture – so it will be a little crumbly when you bring the dough together: be confident and it will coalesce.

Serves 12–16

100g (3½oz) caster (superfine) sugar, or use Korean mint sugar (page 106) and omit the herb below

2 dried fig leaves, or 15 lemon verbena leaves or 12 lavender flowers, broken into florets, or 8 pineapple sage leaves

200g (7oz) unsalted butter

300g (10oz) plain (all purpose) flour

pinch of salt

Preheat the oven to 160°C/325°F/gas mark 3.

Blitz 75g (2½oz) of the sugar with the herb in a coffee grinder or pound in a pestle and mortar. Try it for flavour: you want it good and bold, but not too strong. When it is, mix in the remaining sugar.

Cream the butter with the herb sugar. Sift in the flour and salt, and combine. Roll out to around 5–7mm (¼in) thick and use a small cookie cutter to create circles of shortbread.

Place the shortbread circles on a baking sheet and cook until just beginning to lightly brown, around 15–20 minutes. They will firm up out of the oven. Sprinkle with a little more sugar and allow to cool for 10 minutes before transferring to a wire rack to cool completely.

DRINKS

TARRAGON AND SALAD BURNET LEMONADE

This is perfect when the fish are jumpin' and the cotton is high. The cucumber wow of salad burnet and tarragon's bold, grassy aniseed make for a bright and breezy reviver, with all the zing you want from a homemade lemonade. If you don't have salad burnet, cucumber might burpily substitute. Treat this as a template for experimentation: ginger rosemary, mint, lemongrass and lemon verbena in any combination will be superb. It's also a bit special with fizz, in cocktails (add a lime, white rum, plenty of ice and soda for a cracking mojito) or just with gin and tonic.

Makes 350ml (12fl oz)

60g (2¼oz) tarragon sprigs

60g (2¼oz) salad burnet

200g (7oz) caster (superfine) sugar

grated zest and juice of 6 unwaxed lemons

Strip the tarragon leaves from the stems; discard the stems. Blitz everything in a high-powered blender until no obvious pieces remain. Pass through a sieve anyway, to remove any tiny pieces that linger.

Dilute to taste – with three or four parts sparkling water.

RASPBERRY AND LEMON THYME SWITCHEL

Switchels and shrubs are fine comings-together of sugar/honey and vinegar. Shrubs are usually fruity fermentations, while switchels are flavoured with herbs or spices, and ready to drink with a little wait.

The classic switchel of honey, lemon and ginger in vinegar became popular in 1800s America, a workplace refresher, also known as Haymaker's Punch, but you don't have to work up a sweat to enjoy this. Lemon verbena, lemongrass and ginger rosemary are excellent variations on the lemon thyme.

Makes about 1 litre (1¾ pints)

20g (¾oz) fresh ginger, peeled and finely chopped

2 tsp lemon juice

70ml (2½fl oz) apple cider vinegar

3 tbsp honey (raw, ideally)

large handful of raspberries

8–10cm (3–4in) sprig of lemon thyme

Add the ginger, lemon juice and vinegar to a 1 litre (1¾ pint) jar and stir to encourage the ginger to release its flavour. Add the honey and stir until dissolved. Add the raspberries, squeezing them slightly as you do. Fill the jar with water, leaving 3cm (1¼in) at the top of the jar. Seal.

Leave this overnight to infuse and to allow the flavours to develop. Add the lemon thyme and allow to infuse for 4 more hours or so, then refrigerate. Pour through a sieve when you want to drink it. It's wonderful as it is, with ice, or with gin.

SHISO, LEMON VERBENA, VIETNAMESE CORIANDER AND CUCUMBER SHRUB

Shrubs are intense combinations of vinegar, sugar and fruit, usually enlivened with herbs and/or spices, and fermented for a short time. You can drink them as a short nip, or lengthen with still or sparkling water (1:5 is a good ratio). Many suit cocktails. They are a pleasure to experiment with: stick with the ratio of sugar to vinegar here and try lightly squished raspberries or blueberries instead of the cucumber, and Thai basil in place of the herbs.

Makes about 300ml (10fl oz)

250g (9oz) caster (superfine) sugar

300ml (10fl oz) white wine vinegar or cider vinegar

15g (½oz) shiso leaves, shredded

8 lemon verbena leaves, shredded

25 Vietnamese coriander leaves, shredded

1 large cucumber, peeled

Dissolve the sugar in the vinegar in a pan over a medium heat, stirring frequently. Take the pan off the heat.

Place all the leaves in a non-reactive bowl and pour the warm, sweet vinegar over. Allow to cool.

Grate the cucumber into the bowl, stir and cover with a tea towel. Leave it to infuse for at least 12 hours, and up to 24.

Pour through a strainer into a jug and decant into a sterilized jar or bottle. You can use it immediately, but it's better off left to mature for a week in the fridge. It will last for 3 weeks or so in the fridge.

ALLORINO

Of the many Biblical tales that were cast at an impervious young me by a squadron of kindly Sunday school nuns, the story of Jesus being tempted by the devil in the Judaean Desert is one of the few that fascinated. His ordeal of restraint lasted 40 days and 40 nights, and here I recreate this period of sufferance not in the search for spiritual nourishment but divine intoxication. The wait is worth it.

The Italian for bay leaf is *foglia d'alloro*, hence this liqueur's name. It may resemble dentist swill when infusing but it matures to a glowing walnut colour, and works perfectly as a room temperature comforter in front of the fire, an icy digestivo at the end of a good meal, or an on-the-rocks summer sizzler with prosecco.

If only all recipes were as memorable, with its many 40s.

Makes just over 1 litre (1¾ pints)

40 bay leaves

700ml (1¼ pints) vodka

300g (10oz) caster (superfine) sugar

Wash the bay leaves and tear them a little to accelerate the infusion process. Add them and the vodka to a large jar (a 1.5 litre/2½ pint Kilner jar is ideal), and leave to infuse for 40 days.

Make a sugar syrup by stirring the sugar into 250ml (9fl oz) simmering water. Turn off the heat and allow to cool for a good 15 minutes, before pouring into the jar: the warmth will reinvigorate the infusion process. Leave for 40 days, then strain into a clean bottle before drinking.

LOVAGE VODKA

I am not infrequently accused of spending a fair proportion of my life submerging bits of herb or fruit in alcohol and dressing it up as work. I offer you this peculiar but excellent infusion as evidence that the time spent in research is at least occasionally fruitful.

This is perfect for Bloody Marys, but also just as it is as a livening nip served stone cold, or with tonic.

I wouldn't leave this to infuse for long, at least the first time you make it; within a couple of days it will be bitterly poky, with the sugar just settling it down a little.

Keep the leaves attached to the stem; there's a pleasing touch of the reverse ship-in-a-bottle about retrieving them.

Makes 700ml (1¼ pints)

700ml (1¼ pints) vodka

150g (5oz) caster (superfine) sugar

20 leaves or so of lovage, still attached to the stem

Half-fill a jar or bottle with vodka and add the sugar using a funnel. Invert and generally agitate to start the sugar dissolving. Add the lovage leaves, top with the remaining vodka, and leave somewhere cool and dark to infuse.

Remove the leaves when it reaches the flavour you want.

LIMONCELLO

If you have been to southern Italy, you may have become enchanted with limoncello, a delightful liqueur, heavy with lemons, usually served cold as divorce, after a meal. You may also have returned home, enthusiastically bought a bottle to relive those hot days away and found supermarket limoncello closer to toilet cleaner than the real deal. This is the antidote. Enjoy cold as a digestivo or (if you intend to sleep where you are sitting) diluted with sparkling wine. (Pictured opposite.)

Makes 1 litre (1¾ pints)

500ml (18fl oz) vodka (or gin if you prefer)

pared zest of 3 unwaxed lemons

2 lemongrass stalks

500g (1lb 2oz) caster (superfine) sugar

3 good sprigs of lemon verbena

Pour the vodka into a 1 litre (1¾ pint) jar, add the lemon zest, lemongrass and stir well. Leave for a week to infuse.

In a large pan over a medium heat, add the sugar to 500ml (18fl oz) water, stirring until it is dissolved. Turn off the heat and allow to cool for 5 minutes. Add the lemon verbena to the vodka, and pour in as much of the warm syrup as will fill the bottle. Once cool, place in the fridge. It will be bright and lively initially, mellowing and deepening in flavour over time: both are excellent.

PINA COLADA MOJITO

I should be calling this 'The Rupert Holmes' but as earworms go, Rupert Holmes' 'Escape' (yes, everyone knows it as the Pina Colada Song) is pretty hard to winkle out once embedded, so I won't.

You can use mint and fennel if you are without Korean mint, or grow anise hyssop, its very close relative, instead. And if, like Rupert, you're not much into health food but are into champagne, you could try fizz instead of rum.

Serves 1

10 leaves of Korean mint (or mint and a few fronds of fennel instead)

4 tbsp white rum

ice

6–7 chunks of pineapple (optional)

4 tbsp fresh pineapple juice

50ml (2fl oz) fig leaf syrup (page 119)

juice of 1 lime

Place the mint in a tall glass and bruise the leaves using the handle of a wooden spoon or a mortar to release the scent and flavour.

Add the rum and ice, then the pineapple (if using), pineapple juice, syrup and lime juice, and stir. Drink while reading the personal ads.

TARRAGON GIMLET

My favourite of the stories as to the origin of this cocktail's name is that Surgeon Admiral Sir Thomas Gimlette apparently added lime to the daily gin allowance of his Royal Navy men in an attempt to ward off scurvy. I can confirm that I have been entirely scurvy-free while drinking this, so bottoms up, for health.

In these quantities, the tarragon doesn't drive a coach and horses through this – it barely reads as itself, just transporting the lime and vodka perfectly. When making the syrup, add generous quantities of tarragon, and go with a ratio of 1.5:1 sugar to water to get sweet tarragon without too much dilution.

Do experiment: gin in place of vodka works differently well, a couple of makrut lime leaves add something intriguing to the tarragon syrup, alter the proportions of vodka to juice to syrup, and should you require something delightfully leisurely rather than a set of jump leads to your core, dilute with tonic to taste. Everything, including the glass, should be as cold as a welldigger's arse. (Pictured opposite.)

Serves 1

4 tbsp vodka
2 tbsp lime juice
2 tbsp tarragon syrup
(page 34)

Add everything plus ice to a cocktail shaker and shake, straining into a suitable glass. If you are without a shaker, use a jar and a sieve.

SAGE AND CITRUS GIMLET

As with the tarragon gimlet, the amounts can be tweaked depending on the intensity of the citrus and the syrup, and the type of gin you favour. These amounts are roughly the juice of half a lime and half a grapefruit. The sage reads late and subtle on the tongue but it's humming quietly in the background, joining the dots with the rest. As easy as this is to drink, it is a proper bolt to the electrical box, though not without elegance; add tonic if you fancy a longer pleasure. Everything should be cold cold cold.

Serves 1

40ml (1½ fl oz) sage syrup
(page 34)
50ml (2fl oz) red grapefruit
juice
2 tbsp lime juice

Add everything plus ice to a cocktail shaker and shake, straining into a suitable glass. If you are without a shaker, use a jar and a sieve.

AUTHOR BIO

Mark is lucky enough to spend most of his time eating, growing, writing and talking about food. His *A Year at Otter Farm* and *A Taste of the Unexpected* both won Food Book of the Year, for André Simon and the Guild of Food Writers, respectively. His most recent book, *Sour*, was shortlisted for the Fortnum & Mason Cookery Book of the Year Award 2020 and the James Beard Foundation Single Subject Book Award 2020, and was *The Sunday Times* and *Daily Mail* Food Book of the Year 2019. Known for growing everything from Szechuan pepper to pecans to Asian pears, Mark's refreshing approach to growing and eating has done much to inspire a new generation to grow some of what they eat. He was involved with River Cottage, appearing in the TV series, running courses and events at River Cottage HQ, and he has written four River Cottage books. Mark also writes regularly for a range of publications including the *Telegraph* and *Country Life*, and his features have appeared in the *Observer*, *Guardian*, *National Geographic*, and others.

SUPPLIERS

Plants and seeds:
Otter Farm – otterfarm.co.uk
Pennard Plants – pennardplants.com
Jekka's – jekkas.com
Plants 4 Presents – plants4presents.co.uk
Sea Spring Seeds – seaspringseeds.co.uk
Victoriana Nursery Gardens – victoriananursery.co.uk
Hooksgreen Herbs – hooksgreenherbs.com

Ingredients:
Go as local as you can for fresh herbs.
Sous Chef – souschef.co.uk
Daphnis and Chloe – daphnisandchloe.com
Persepolis – foratasteofpersia.co.uk
The Spice Shop – thespiceshop.co.uk

INDEX

ACKNOWLEDGEMENTS

I am wildly lucky to have had such a creative, energetic and dedicated team to work with on this book. That they have all brought those qualities during a time when it has been largely impossible to meet in person is extraordinary.

Thanks to:
Sarah Lavelle, for brilliantly overseeing such a great collection of food writers at Quadrille and including me in their number; it is a pleasure to work with you. Harriet Webster, editor, for your skill, energy, humour and light touch in making this book what it is. Claire Rochford, Head of Design: once again, you were (almost) always right, and to such great effect. Matt Cox, designer extraordinaire – a joy to work with you again. Tatiana Boyko, whose beautiful illustrations for the cover capture the spirit of the book. Clare Sayer, for your excellent and sensitive copy editing. Sally Somers for your careful proofreading. Matt Williamson – unquestionably the rudest man I know, and that is saying something – for working with me on almost half of the recipes, and your usual brilliance on the photoshoots. Becky Smedley, Emma Marijewycz, Laura Willis and Laura Eldridge, and the entire sales team at Quadrille, for your dedicated and enthusiastic work in helping it fly.

To Chris, Mike and Jayne at the nursery, and to Lia, Diana, Catherine and Cathy for, in one way or another, adding to the book.

To my agent, Caroline Michel at PFD, who is the embodiment of enthusiastic support and guidance; and to Laurie Robertson, also at PFD: thank you.

Thank you all for making what is apparently work seem like solely a pleasure.